IMMIGRATION
AND THE
NEXT
AMERICA

IMMIGRATION
AND THE
NEXT
AMERICA

Renewing the Soul of Our Nation

ARCHBISHOP
JOSÉ H. GOMEZ

OUR SUNDAY VISITOR PUBLISHING DIVISION
OUR SUNDAY VISITOR, INC.
HUNTINGTON, INDIANA 46750

Cover design: Tyler Ottinger
Cover art: Shutterstock
Interior design: Lindsey Riesen

PRINTED IN THE UNITED STATES OF AMERICA

To Pope Francis,
an immigrant's son and the first pope
from the New World

CONTENTS

ONE

THE NEXT AMERICA

Our national debate about immigration has reached a crossroads. For more than a decade, we have basically been defaulting on this issue.

Although no one knows the exact number, it is estimated that about eleven million people are living in this country without our government's permission. Some crossed our borders without first getting a visa from our government. Others came in through proper channels but decided to stay after their visas or other temporary permits ran out.

Either way, they are considered "illegal immigrants." And their numbers — and the fears and anger surrounding their presence — have caused a growing crisis in American life.

Each year states are passing tougher anti-immigrant laws — nearly 270 in 2012 and more than 300 the year before that, according to the National Conference of State Legislatures. Practically, it's hard to see how most of these measures contribute to solving actual problems. Many seem vindictive, as if their intent is to injure and intimidate. But the mood has been angry, and there is a lot of feeling that we need to do *something*.

On the national level, our immigration policy has also been focused on punishing illegal immigrants. Here, too, we see signs of desperation and moral confusion. Many of our leaders seriously believe the issue can best be "solved" by rounding up and removing everyone caught living in our midst without proper legal documents. This would be a human rights nightmare — involving the forced repatriation of a population roughly the size of Ohio, the country's seventh largest state. But this is seriously argued, and over the last four years our government has steadily pursued this policy course, deporting at least 1.5 million people — 400,000 in 2012 alone, a record number.

Our political speech these days expresses the disorder of our public moral reasoning, as we try to justify what can't be justified. Politicians talk in euphemisms about a policy goal they call "enforcement by attrition." What they mean is this: making life so scary and harsh for people who are here illegally that they will want to leave the country of their own accord.

From the courts and legislatures to the media and popular opinion, there is an outraged, personal tone to our immigration debate that you don't hear very often in our politics.

Even ordinary Americans seem to feel they have been pushed to the edge. These are good people and good citizens. They are small business owners, entrepreneurs, employers, parents, and political leaders in their communities. These are people of religious faith and moral conviction who love their families and love their country, and are generous with their time and money. They are worried about where America is headed. And with good cause.

Most of the time, most of the arguments in our public debate are motivated by patriotic ideals and concern for the common good. But there is a persistent undertone that cannot be mistaken. It is driven by fear and, sadly, also by chauvinism. A lot of people — a lot of good Christian people — are saying things they know they shouldn't be saying about a category of men and women they have never talked to, only talked about. A category of people they have reduced to an abstract enemy they identify as "illegals."

I can understand the anger and resentment surrounding this issue. I don't like to see our laws disregarded either. America has always been a nation of laws. Writing at our nation's founding, Thomas Paine, in *Common Sense* (1776), said, "In America, law is king." Harvard's Mary Ann Glendon is correct when she says there is "no country on earth where legal values play a more prominent role in the nation's conception of itself than the United States."

The presence in our midst of millions of unauthorized immigrants offends something deep in our American self-understanding. The chaos that illegal immigration has caused in some of our southern border communities only adds to a general feeling of lawlessness. The thought that these immigrants might go unpunished or win some kind of amnesty strikes at our basic sensibilities of justice and fair play.

Anger often feeds on fear, and there is also a lot of fear at work in our debate. The fear is that perhaps our government doesn't have as much control over our borders or our social order as we want to believe. These fears are stirred up by loud voices warning that America is in decline, and that illegal immigration is an invasion that threatens to make us an "alien nation."

I have my own fear. My fear is that in our frustration and anger, we are losing our grip and perspective. If you allow me to say this as a pastor: I'm worried we are losing something of our national soul.

America is a great nation: free and prosperous, brave and generous. Throughout our history and still today, Americans have been willing to sacrifice, even to lay down our lives, for others in need. At home and abroad. In times of war, and in times of peace. Americans can be found wherever people are poor and suffering — lending a hand, saving lives, building communities, bringing people hope.

Yet this great nation finds itself today reduced to addressing this major issue in our public life through name calling and discrimination, "profiling" based on race, random identity checks, commando-style raids of workplaces and homes, arbitrary detentions and deportations.

We seem almost willfully blind to the fact that illegal immigration is no ordinary crime.

The fact is that most "illegals" are the people next door. They go to work every day. Their kids go to school with our kids. We sit next to them at church on Sunday. Most have been living in our country for five years or more. Two-thirds have been here for at least a decade.

According to the Pew Hispanic Center, nearly half of all illegal immigrants are living in homes with a spouse and children.

More than 5 million children are growing up in homes with one or more illegal parents — and about 80 percent of these kids are American citizens, born in this country.

These are the realities that make our response to this crime so cruel. For all its limitations, our national immigration policy has always tried to keep parents and children together and to reunite families that are separated by our borders. Not anymore.

In the name of enforcing our laws, now we are breaking up families. One in four deportees are being removed from an intact family. We are talking about souls, not statistics. We are talking about families. We're talking about fathers and husbands who, with no warning, will not be coming home for dinner tonight — and who may not see their families again for a decade at least. We are talking about women suddenly left as single mothers to raise their children in poverty. We are talking about a state policy that results in making many children virtually "orphans," to be raised on the streets or in foster care.

What are we doing? To these kids and to ourselves? Who are we becoming? Since when has America become a nation that punishes innocent children for the sins of their parents?

This is what the immigration issue is doing to our national soul. We need to stop ourselves. We can do better. America has always been a nation of justice and law. But we are also a people of compassion and common sense. What we're doing right now betrays our values and makes our country weaker and more vulnerable.

We are a better people than this. We can find a better way.

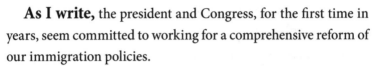

As I write, the president and Congress, for the first time in years, seem committed to working for a comprehensive reform of our immigration policies.

This is very encouraging to me. Immigration is a national issue. It's about our national security, about who we allow into our country and why. This should not be a matter for individual states to decide. But the states have been forced to act because for too long the federal government has abdicated its duties. The lack of courage and failure of leadership on immigration has been widespread and cuts across party lines.

It's no wonder people are frustrated. There has been no meaningful movement at the federal level since comprehensive reform legislation failed in Congress in 2007. The costs of inaction have been cruel and ongoing — for the millions of illegal immigrants and their families, and for millions of ordinary Americans, especially those living in border states.

We say we are worried about the long-term social costs of illegal immigration. If we are, then we should be looking for every way possible to integrate the undocumented into our economy so that they do not become a permanent underclass of dependent people. Our policy today, unfortunately, is only helping that underclass grow in numbers. The underclass grows every time we break apart a family by deporting a working father and leaving women and children behind in poverty. We are creating the very conditions that we claim to be afraid of — a generation of people who can't assimilate and who don't have the education and skills to contribute to our economy.

So I am hopeful the president and Congress can come together to create a principled policy that welcomes newcomers who have the character and skills our country needs to flourish and grow; a policy that secures our borders against illegal crossings and lets us keep track of those who are already living within our borders; a policy that includes a just solution to the questions raised by those who are here in violation of our laws and produces a path for them to make restitution and become citizens; a policy we can enforce with fairness and mercy.

Reforms in these areas would make a big difference in the lives of millions of people. We need these kinds of reforms if America is going to compete in a global economy at a time when our domestic workforce is shrinking and our population is aging. But immigration reform is about more than finding technical solutions. If immigration was only about fixing a broken system, the system would have been fixed already.

That's why I decided to write this little book in the middle of this debate: Because immigration is about more than immigration.

I'm concerned that the deeper issues at stake in this debate are being ignored and will be left undiscussed, while politicians, labor unions and businesses focus on forging the compromises needed to address the political issues. If this turns out to be the case, it will be more than a missed opportunity. I'm convinced that unless we address these underlying issues, any reform enacted may be only partial and unsustainable, leading to even more injustices and resentments down the road.

If the promise of immigration reform is to succeed in the long run, then we should make this debate a time for soul-searching

— both for our nation and for each one of us as citizens. So in the pages that follow, I want to try to think through some of these deeper issues. I believe the question of immigration goes to the heart of America's identity and our future as a nation. We can't truly resolve the political issues of immigration unless we have some common agreement or shared understanding about our country's identity and purpose.

I write not as a politician but as a pastor. I'm a Catholic priest and a bishop. I write as a Catholic and also as a proud naturalized American citizen. I was born in Monterrey, Mexico, and I did not come to this country to live until I was in my thirties. So I am an immigrant. My people come from both Mexico and America. I was raised in Monterrey, but I have relatives who have been in what's now Texas since 1805, when it was still under Spanish rule. I still have family on both sides of the U.S.-Mexico border.

My experience is hardly unique. The Catholic Church in this country has always been a Church of immigrants, just as America has always been a nation of immigrants. Nearly all of us can trace our genealogy beyond our borders to some foreign land where we or our ancestors came from. Catholics make up the largest religious tradition in our population, and we reflect the beautiful diversity of our nation. The Catholic Church in America is a spiritual family drawn from some sixty ethnic and national groups from every continent.

The word "catholic" means "universal" or, literally, "embracing the whole universe." And you can really feel that in Los Angeles, where I serve as the archbishop. Los Angeles is the nation's largest Catholic community, and we are Korean and Italian, Chinese and Japanese, Indian and Filipino, Native American and Samoan, Vietnamese and Irish, Armenian and African, black and Hispanic. In Los Angeles, we worship and carry out our ministries in forty-two languages.

So immigration policy and the underlying issues in our immigration debate are matters of deep concern to me — personally, and also as a Catholic leader and American citizen.

The Catholic Church does not have an immigration policy or technical solutions to offer. Neither do I. But through our charities, ministries, schools, and parishes, the Church has far more day-to-day experience with immigrants — documented and undocumented — than any other institution in American public life. I believe this experience, and the Church's teachings on human dignity and social justice, can contribute a great deal to our thinking about this issue.

Politics is a conversation about how we ought to order our lives together. At least that's what politics should be. But in order to have that conversation, we need to agree on basic terms. In order to know what we *ought* to do, we need to have some shared understanding of our past and the historical project of this great nation.

We need to be thinking about the American story and who we are meant to be as a people. We need to know where we've been, where we're at, and what direction we should take. These are the questions for our nation. And these are the questions for each one of us who wants to be a faithful citizen at this moment in our national history.

Immigration is about more than immigration. It always has been.

The question of immigration is a question about America. About our national identity and destiny. What is America? What does it mean to be an American? Who are we as a people and where are we heading as a country? What will the "next America" look like? What *should* the next America look like?

Our debate over immigration reform reflects the deep anxieties that many Americans feel about these questions — about the state of the nation and our future. Many of us see our country changing, and we are troubled by what we see. We sense that the forces driving these changes — forces both inside and outside our borders — have been at work for a long time. Somehow we feel that we're traveling on the wrong track. We see the next America coming, and it worries us.

Immigration has become a kind of flash point for these deeper anxieties we have about America's future.

Our anxiety on immigration reflects, first of all, our worries about our national sovereignty and security. A decade after the terrorist attacks of September 11, 2001, we still feel threatened and vulnerable. We know those attacks were conceived and carried out by foreigners living among us with ties to enemies overseas. That scares us. As it should.

When we see violence and lawlessness caused by drug cartels in our near neighbor, Mexico, that makes us even more worried about border security and the kinds of people who might get into our country. Then bombs go off at the Boston Marathon apparently planted and detonated by two immigrants. So we are afraid for our safety. In approaching immigration, we are determined to make sure that people who want to hurt us will never get across our borders again. We want walls and assurances.

Not only do we feel exposed to a future terrorist attack. Our sovereignty and security are threatened by an increasingly globalized economy and financial system, spurred by communications technologies and the Internet.

More and more we realize that what we produce and how we work, what we earn and our standards of living, are all tied to technologies and powers we cannot control. We understand that transnational corporations and financial institutions, foreign currency markets, and political events in places we will never see, are determining our lives and livelihoods.

The immigration issue is a product of the processes of economic globalization and internationalization. Widespread migration is one of the chief signs of our times. It's not simply limited to the United States and the Americas. It's a global phenomenon. According to the International Organization for Migration, there are about 214 million international migrants worldwide.

In general, people migrate for either political or economic reasons. In the Western Hemisphere, the reasons are mostly economic. People are not so much fleeing tyranny or persecution as they are seeking jobs and a better future for their families.

Globalization has changed the way businesses operate and the way people work. Owners of businesses no longer make their products locally for domestic markets. Now their production facilities are located all over the world. The markets for their products are likewise international. Even small farmers and small businesses now find they are competing in a worldwide market.

The new realities of global production and competition, along with the globalization of money and capital, have led to radical changes in the labor market. Workers no longer compete for jobs only with their fellow countrymen. Now workers in one country are competing for jobs with workers in other countries around the world. Wages and benefits paid in other countries drive wages and benefits in our country.

Globalization has expanded opportunities for businesses and for workers. But it has also created many problems. One problem is that while we have developed laws and policies to govern the flow of capital and money, we have no standards for the movement of laborers.

For instance, NAFTA, the North American Free Trade Agreement of 1994, eliminated tariffs and many restrictions on trade and business in the United States, Mexico, and Canada. It did not include provisions concerning the mobility of persons. The result is that money, capital, and other resources now flow more freely among our three nations, but human beings — the men and women who do the work — cannot. In the new economy, there are many safeguards for businesses and financial institutions, but few for workers.

Globalization has exposed, and in some cases made worse, the economic inequalities and injustices that exist within and between nations. These inequalities — the poverty in which so many of our people live — are the root causes of immigration. People leave their homes and their families because they are needy and desperate. They leave their home countries because they cannot provide the necessities of life for themselves and their families.

This situation will not change until we address economic inequalities in the Americas. As long as workers can earn more in one hour in the United States than they can earn in a day or a week in Mexico and the rest of Latin America, they'll keep coming to this country for work.

In recent years, our insecurity has been heightened by the global recession and instability in world financial markets. Millions are still out of work across America. Many of our cities and states are in deep fiscal trouble. Immigration becomes part of larger debates we are having across the country — about the role and reach of government, and about welfare programs, taxes, unions, and public debt.

Nowadays we're thinking that the time when rising tides could lift all boats has passed. America, we feel, has entered a new era of scarcity and diminished opportunity. We question whether we have the resources to support new immigrants. We worry that immigrants will take our jobs or lower our wages. We do the math, and it doesn't add up. We figure that what immigrants contribute in hard work and taxes will be outweighed by the burden they will impose on our already strained social services networks.

So we are worried about globalization and the threat of terrorism. We are also troubled by demographic changes we see taking place inside America.

Demographics experts measure fertility — the number of children a woman will bear during the course of her lifetime. They also measure birthrates — the number of children born for every 1,000 people per year. Both measures are dropping dramatically in our country. The experts can suggest many possible reasons for this — more educational and workplace opportunities for women; better health care; easier access to birth control, abortion, and divorce.

Whatever the reason, the demographic reality is that Americans are having fewer children and are living longer. Our population is getting older, and at the same time the pool of American-born workers is shrinking. Already we are seeing pressures on our social welfare system.

That's because our social welfare system is founded on a set of calculations related to a simple demographic assumption — that there will be a steady stream of young people entering the workforce; that these workers will pay taxes into the system; and that those tax monies will then be used to fund Medicaid, Medicare, Social Security, and other social assistance programs.

Today, that model is breaking down under the weight of demographic pressures. Far more workers are retiring from the workforce than there are younger workers entering the workforce. We have more people dependent on social services than we have working to support them. This raises large questions about how our government will meet our obligations to those who are too old, too sick, or who are otherwise unable to work.

America's situation is not as bad as it is in other parts of the developed world that have more extensive state-run welfare systems. In some countries in Europe, for instance, the birthrates are so low and social needs so high that governments are essentially trying to pay young couples to have more children.

As these trends have been quietly going on, America's ethnic and racial profile has also been changing. Last year, for the first time in our history, white Americans — those who trace their ancestry to the nations of Europe — accounted for less than half of the new children born in the United States. In other words, minority babies, for the first time, were the majority of the babies born in America.

We have been seeing this reality in the Catholic Church for many years. We measure demographics by the number of babies we are baptizing each year. In Los Angeles, we have been baptizing on average about 84,000 newborns and infants each year — the majority of them are children of Latinos, Asians, and other non-white parents.

To give some perspective on these numbers — and also to indicate how the nation's demographic center of gravity is shifting from the North and East to the South and West: infant baptisms in the nation's second and third largest Catholic communities — New York and Chicago — *combined* are averaging around 63,000 in recent years.

What we are seeing in the Church is true for the nation as a whole. According to the latest census, about 13 percent of Americans are now foreign-born. There are four states now where racial and ethnic minorities outnumber Americans of European descent, all of them in the West — Hawaii, New Mexico, Texas, and California. Ethnic minorities are the majority now in six of America's ten largest cities.

Hispanics make up 16 percent of all Americans today. And that percentage will only continue to grow. Nearly one-quarter of American children age 17 and under is Hispanic.

The point of these statistics is that America's "face" is being changed forever. The patterns suggest that the next America will be less and less white European and more and more Latino and Asian.

In the immigration debate we can see that these demographic changes are a source of deep apprehension. Many of us are fearful and uncertain about the growing presence of neighbors who don't look like us, who speak different languages, and who have different traditions and countries of origin.

There is one final factor that I think is contributing to our unease about the future: a fear that America is losing its sense of national identity and the meaning of citizenship.

For most of our history, there has been an unspoken consensus that America was "one nation under God," with an exceptional identity and responsibility among the family of nations. For most of our history, we were confident that American institutions should shape moral character and instill the civic virtues required for our democracy to function. Virtues such as religion and family; individual freedom and responsibility; the work ethic; the rule of law; equality of opportunity; honesty, fair play, and the common good; the sense of politics as public service.

Today, this moral consensus no longer holds. We see many signs that traditional American values and civic virtues are losing their importance.

We could point to almost every area of American life. We could talk about the moral and intellectual decadence of elite groups or the rise of short-term opportunism in business and finance. We could talk about the widening economic and cultural divides between the wealthiest and poorest Americans. We could talk about a political system that has become increasingly bitter, ineffective, and driven by special interests. We could talk about the crazed consumerism of our economy, which presents entertainment and pleasure-seeking as the highest reasons for living.

America is becoming a different country.

We are now a country where about a million children have been killed in the womb *each year for the last 40 years.* In some places in our country, more children die by abortion than are born each year. America is now a country where four of every ten children are born to mothers who are not married. Confusion over the meaning of marriage, family, and sexuality is widespread in public policy and personal practice. We are a country where the killing of the old and sick is legal in several states and increasingly accepted in our laws and public opinion.

These trends coincide with America's spiritual decline, reflected in the growing secularization of our society.

Our nation's founding documents express faith in a Creator who endows men and women with "unalienable" rights. But, today, we're living in an America where more and more of our neighbors go through their daily lives without even thinking about God. Our country's fastest growing belief system is "no religion." Millions are living as if there is no God, or as if his existence doesn't make any difference.

America's founders understood that our democracy's strength depends on our citizens' freedom to live according to their faith and moral principles. But, today, believers confront relentless legal and cultural pressures to keep their religion to themselves.

Many of our leaders today — in government, higher education, media, and culture — express frank hostility toward religious people and their aspirations and institutions. If people of faith want to take part in our country's economic, political, and cultural life, we are forced to act as if our beliefs don't make any difference in how we live or how we carry out our duties as employers, employees, neighbors, or citizens.

These developments in our civic life are deeply troubling. Taken together, they suggest that American identity is now so totally fragmented that we no longer share any values and attachments that can draw us together as one people. Indeed, many of our leaders and educators seem to reject the idea that there are common "American" values or duties that should be taught or expected of citizens and others living here.

I sense that many opponents of immigration reform "get" this negative drift in our civic consciousness and public morality. They understand that immigration requires integration or what used to be described, without irony, as Americanization. They understand that if immigration is to succeed and make our country stronger, we need an "identity kit" — a set of values, attachments, and expectations — to pass on to those who want to become citizens.

Many of us wonder — and with good cause — if we have lost our faith in a common American identity. What's left to build on that transcends self-interests or group interests? Beyond buying the same products, rooting for the same teams, or watching the same shows on television, is there anything that Americans have in common anymore? Is there anything that makes us one people? Or are we just a collection of individuals with different identities based on our cultural and ethnic backgrounds or lifestyle choices?

Immigration is about more than immigration. Immigration is caught up in these deeper questions about the next America.

America is becoming a fundamentally different country. Deep down, we understand this. So immigration has become a kind of line in the sand that we are drawing. We seem to be saying "here and no further" until we address these deeper questions. We are making immigrants, especially the undocumented ones, into a kind of symbol of all these factors that we are worried about. That's one reason I don't think it's possible to resolve the immigration issue only by making technical improvements to our policy mechanisms.

Over the past several years, I've talked to many Americans, and I've listened carefully to their arguments against immigration. I have to say: I have a lot of sympathy for their point of view. I understand why they want to build more walls to secure our borders. I agree when they say we should look more closely at who we let into our country. Opponents of immigration are trying to express something admirable and patriotic. They are trying to defend this country that they love.

This is a beautiful desire. It's a desire that I share. But I find myself wondering — what America are we talking about? The dream of America — America as it was founded to be — is not the reality anymore. It hasn't been for quite some time. The America we love and want to protect does not exist anymore. America is moving in disturbing and uncharted directions. It's time for all of us to acknowledge this — no matter what our position is on the political issues of immigration.

Immigration is about more than immigration. It's also about American renewal. Immigration is a human rights test of our generation. It's also a defining historical moment for America.

The meaning of this moment is that we need to make the next America a new America. An America renewed in the image of her founding promises of universal rights rooted in God and not in blood or race. This needs to be a moment of national renewal and self-reflection. It is not a time for detachment.

As Americans, we all need to pray and work together for the common good of our nation. If we are religious believers, we need to live the truths of our faith. We need to look at these issues, not from the self-interested perspectives of politics, but from God's point of view — and with an eye toward what he requires of us.

If the next America is to become the new America, we need a new narrative — a new appreciation of American history that can sustain us on our national journey. I have become convinced that one of our biggest problems today is that America has lost her national "story." We don't know anymore where America came from and what makes this country unique. We have lost the sense of our nation's purpose and who we are meant to be as a people.

What is America's national character, and what is our mission in the world? What does it mean to be an American in the twenty-first century, really? Do any of these questions even make sense to us anymore?

Two

THE GREATER AMERICA

I have strong memories of the 1960 presidential election in the United States. I remember the pride I felt when I learned that John F. Kennedy had been elected. Even an eight-year-old boy in Monterrey, Mexico, could understand that something important was happening with our neighbors just a few hours to the north. After more than a century of anti-immigrant and anti-Catholic discrimination, America had finally elected an Irish Catholic as president.

The 1960 election was a sign of the deep capacities for conversion and renewal in the American democratic system. For many, that era still evokes a time when there was a sense of passion, possibility, and purpose in our politics, qualities that nowadays seem to be lacking.

Most of us have forgotten that immigration reform was a key to President Kennedy's agenda for the nation. In fact, the only book he wrote on public policy was called *A Nation of Immigrants*. In one of his last acts as president, just three months before he was assassinated, he proposed comprehensive immigration reform legislation to Congress. His plan became the basis for the 1965 Immigration and Nationality Act, which is the foundation of American policy still today.

I was reading *A Nation of Immigrants* again recently. It's a good book, and definitely written with an agenda. President Kennedy is angry about anti-immigrant prejudice. At one point he makes a bitter allusion to the famous poem on the Statue of Liberty which promises the world, "give me your tired, your poor, your huddled masses yearning to breathe free." America's actual policies, Kennedy charges, only welcome immigrants "as long as they come from Northern Europe, are not too tired or too poor or slightly ill, never stole a loaf of bread, never joined a questionable organization, and can document their activities for the past two years."

Kennedy is most angry about immigration quotas and racial preferences that he says betray America's heritage and ideals. But most of this little book is a simple narrative of how our country was born and how it grew through the contributions of diverse peoples who came here from the ends of the earth seeking liberty and the "American dream."

The last lines of *A Nation of Immigrants* are worth reflecting on.

> Immigration policy should be generous; it
> should be fair; it should be flexible. With such
> a policy we can turn to the world, and to our

past, with clean hands and a clear conscience. Such a policy would be but a reaffirmation of old principles. It would be an expression of our agreement with George Washington that, "The bosom of America is open to receive not only the opulent and respectable stranger, but the oppressed and persecuted of all nations and religions; whom we shall welcome to a participation of all our rights and privileges, if by decency and propriety of conduct they appear to merit the enjoyment."

A Nation of Immigrants was written for a different time and a different America. But almost 60 years later, it should be essential reading for our debates today.

President Kennedy reminds us that welcoming "strangers" has been a defining mark of the American experience beginning with the Declaration of Independence. Among the grievances against King George III, America's founders complained that he was restricting immigration — that he wouldn't allow "the naturalization of foreigners" or "encourage their migrations." America's first president, in his final Thanksgiving Day proclamation, prayed that God would make this country "more and more, a propitious asylum for the unfortunate of other countries."

Our founders' experience as colonists and the principles of their Declaration of Independence have always made America a hospitable destination for foreigners and the world's unfortunates. As a result, America has grown up as "not merely a nation, but a teeming nation of nations," as the poet Walt Whitman wrote in his preface to *Leaves of Grass* (1855).

Nearly all of us today are immigrants by blood. But as President Kennedy reminded us, our commitment to immigration is an obligation of our national spirit that must be renewed in each generation. America's self-identity, as well as our relationship with other nations, depends on our attitude toward immigration. If we turn our back on our history, if we abandon what he called our "old principles," then something in the American spirit will have died.

As important as Kennedy's book is, as I was reading *A Nation of Immigrants* I kept thinking — something is missing. The story he tells about America starts too late — more than a century too late.

President Kennedy begins his story in 1607 with the establishment of Jamestown, America's first permanent English colony. It's a familiar starting point. That's how American history is usually told. The American founding story that most of us know is an Anglo-Protestant tale set in the Northeast and mid-Atlantic states — in Massachusetts, Philadelphia and Virginia. It's the story of the Pilgrims and the *Mayflower,* Plymouth Rock and the first Thanksgiving, and John Winthrop's sermon about a "city upon a hill."

The heroes of this story are politicians and statesmen — Washington, Jefferson, Franklin, Adams. It's the story of high principles and big philosophical ideas — liberty, equality, democracy, individual rights. It's the story of the drafting of great documents — the Declaration of Independence, the Constitution, and the Bill of Rights.

This story of America's beginnings is beautiful. It's also true. Every American should know these characters, and the ideals and principles they fought for. From this story we learn that our American identity and culture are rooted in essentially Christian convictions about the equality and dignity of the human person. But the story of the Pilgrims and the Founding Fathers, and the truths they held to be self-evident, is not the whole story about America.

The rest of the story begins in the 1520s in Florida, and in the 1540s in California, not long after the 1492 voyage of Cristóbal Colón, whom we know as Christopher Columbus. The rest of the story is not a story of colonial settlement but of missionary migration. It's the story of exploration and evangelization. This story is not Anglo-Protestant but Hispanic-Catholic. It is centered not in New England but in *Nueva España* — the New Spain.

To know this other side of America's founding story is to enter into the heart and soul of the Age of Discovery and Christian mission in the late-fifteenth and sixteenth centuries.

This period has been remembered much differently by many of those writing in recent years on history and theology. It is remembered mostly as a chronicle of worldly greed and cruel conquest. The Mexican historian Edmundo O'Gorman said that America was not *discovered* but *invented*. He meant that in a highly critical way. The Mexican American theologian Father Virgilio Elizondo says 1492 started a "Calvary of avarice and misery" for America's indigenous peoples.

Of course, there is a lot of truth in these descriptions. There is no end to the violence and hypocrisy that can be identified at any stage of human history. This period is no exception. Sadly, we know that many came to America not to share their faith but to plunder. The atrocities of the conquerors and their victims' sufferings are all in evidence.

We should feel remorse for these crimes of our history and commit ourselves to learning from them. The problem is that in recent years we have focused too much on documenting victimization and criticizing our ancestors. As a result, we have lost a crucial thread to our national story.

We have lost sight of the fact that the deepest motivations for America's founding were religious and spiritual. We need to recover this lost thread to our story — especially if we want to understand the deeper questions at stake in our immigration debate, the questions of American self-identity.

Christians think about history in light of God's plan for creation. In his classic, *City of God,* Saint Augustine said: "God can never be believed to have left the kingdoms of men, their dominations and their servitudes, outside of the laws of his Providence."

America's Declaration of Independence reflects this way of thinking. It begins with the Founding Fathers professing that the "course of human events" unfolds within "the laws of nature and of nature's God." It concludes with the Founders entrusting their revolution to "the protection of divine Providence."

We don't need to personally believe that God has a plan for history in order to understand America. But we need to recognize that America was founded by people who did in fact hold this belief. To understand the country they set out to create, to understand the America we inherit as their legacy, we need to take their beliefs seriously.

America was born from the Christian mission. This is not an article of faith or a pious wish. It's historical fact. This nation was discovered as part of the great commission that Jesus Christ gave to his Church — to proclaim his Gospel to every nation. Jesus' first apostles carried his Gospel from Galilee and Jerusalem throughout Europe, Africa, and Asia. Centuries later their successors, the popes and bishops, sent missionaries from Spain to the Americas.

The first patents issued to explore the New World don't speak about searching for gold or cheap labor or markets for Spanish goods. They speak about evangelization — sharing the "good news" about Jesus Christ.

The Spanish explorer Lucas Vázquez de Ayllón established the first permanent settlement in North America at San Miguel de Gualdape in 1526, some 80 years before the English established Jamestown. The settlement didn't last long, but its purpose was clear. The patent he received from the King of Spain read:

> The principal intent in the discovery of new
> lands is that the inhabitants and the natives
> thereof ... may be brought to understand the

truth of our holy Catholic faith, that they may
… become Christians and be saved.

This history is important in our current debates because it reminds us that before we were a nation of immigrants, we were a nation founded by missionaries. Two centuries before our founding documents were written down in English, there were immigrants here praying and preaching in Spanish.

We need to know where America came from if we are going to create a future worthy of this great nation. We need to enter into the worldview of those Christians who were the first to come to these shores. We need to recover the sense of mystery they felt about this new land.

There was a utopian, millennial feeling in the air about the mission to America. You find this mystical sense in the *Libro de las Profecias* (*"Book of the Prophecies"*) that Columbus compiled in 1502, ten years after his first voyage. "God made me the messenger of the new heaven and the new earth of which he spoke in the Apocalypse of Saint John … and he showed me the spot where to find it," Columbus wrote.

This same sense of spiritual expectation is present in Amerigo Vespucci's writings. He is the man America is named for, a friend of Columbus, and also an explorer. He was the first to call these lands *Mundus Novus*, the "New World."

Throughout the sixteenth century, Spanish Catholic mystics

stirred the desire to bring the Gospel across the ocean. A cloistered Spanish nun, Venerable María de Ágreda, reported being transported in the spirit more than 500 times to New Mexico, Arizona, and West Texas. Natives in those regions later testified to missionaries that a "lady in blue" who taught them about Jesus had visited them. They said she spoke in Spanish, but they understood it in their native tongue.

María de Ágreda wrote a letter in 1631 that inspired a generation of missionaries, including Blessed Junípero Serra, the Apostle of California, who carried only her writings and a Bible with him to the New World. She wrote:

> For the Divine Majesty appoints you his
> treasurers and disbursers of his Precious Blood
> and places in your hands what it can purchase
> — which is the souls of so many Indians. ...
> Exercise the greatest possible charity with these
> creatures of the Lord, made in his image and
> likeness with a rational soul in order to enable
> them to know him.

Another Spanish mystic, the influential Saint Teresa of Ávila, wept and did penance for the "many millions of souls that were being lost [in the America's] for want of Christian instruction." She inspired others with her praise for the bravery and sacrifice of those missionaries "who, for the love of Our Lord, were able to be engaged in winning souls."

There is a remarkable painting that missionaries made in Peru in the 1650s, called "Allegorical Flotilla of Salvation." It depicts

Saint Joseph, the earthly father of Jesus, leading three golden ships to the New World. The Crucified Christ is also in the picture. His cross serves as a mast for the middle boat. The Virgin Mary flanks him on one side. On the other side is the mystic of the missionaries, Teresa of Ávila.

At its first beginnings, America was conceived as a spiritual project. Many felt the New World was part of the Age of the Holy Spirit foretold by the controversial Franciscan visionary Joachim of Fiore. The missionaries and their sponsors believed that evangelizing these lands would inaugurate what Jesus himself called *the New World* — the close of the age when he would deliver the Kingdom to his Father and come to reign forever over heaven and earth as the King of Kings and Lord of Lords.

Even Shakespeare was caught up in the excitement: "O brave new world, that has such people in't," one of his characters exclaims in *The Tempest* (1611).

The Christian mission to this brave new world was marked by many events that resist our categories of explanation. The greatest of these was the miraculous appearance of the Mother of Jesus Christ on Tepeyac Hill, outside Mexico City, for three days beginning December 9, 1531. To my mind, this apparition is the true spiritual foundation of America — and of all the nations of the Americas, North and South.

There is a long backstory to this drama. The first missionaries came to Mexico in 1522, within five years of Mexico's discovery and Hernán Cortés' conquests of the Aztecs. Almost from the beginning, the missionaries clashed with the corrupt colonial government, which was stealing the natives' property, enslaving women and children, and forcing the proud Náhuatl people into cruel servitude.

The first bishop of Mexico City, a Franciscan friar named Juan de Zumárraga, preached against the brutality. He wrote a long letter urging the Emperor King Carlos V to intervene. But he had no effect. The Spanish conquest provoked deep trauma for the Náhuatl. In 1531, when the land was suddenly visited with a series of unusual natural events — earthquakes, a solar eclipse, and the appearance of Halley's comet — they believed their world was about to come to an end.

Near the end of that year, during the winter solstice, the Mother of Christ appeared. It was a Saturday morning, not yet dawn, and a local man, Juan Diego, was heading off to his catechism class, which was taught every week by a local priest. Juan was one of the first Náhuatl converts to Christianity. As he made his way over the hill, he heard a sound like the singing of birds. And then he saw her — a beautiful maiden with the face of a *mestiza,* with both Spanish and native features.

And this beautiful woman said to him:

> I am honored to be your compassionate
> Mother!
> Your mother and the mother of all the people
> that live together in this land.
> I am also the Mother of all the other various
> lineages of men and women —

those who love me, those who cry to me,
those who seek me, those who trust in me.

The mysterious woman instructed Juan to ask the bishop to build a church on Tepeyac Hill. Not surprisingly, Bishop Zumárraga demanded some evidence that the apparition was real. But neither he nor anybody else could have expected the "proof" he received.

Three days later, Juan told the maiden about the bishop's skepticism. So she presented Juan with a large bouquet of roses. This was unusual because roses do not bloom in Mexico in December. The Virgin told Juan to bring the bouquet to the bishop.

Juan did what she told him. He wrapped the roses up in his cloak, called a *tilma*, and he brought them back to the bishop. When he arrived and opened his cloak, Juan and the bishop were both amazed to find not the roses but a beautiful image of the maiden imprinted on the inside of Juan's *tilma*.

Saint Juan Diego's miraculous *tilma* still hangs in the Basilica of Our Lady of Guadalupe in Mexico City. Scientists have never been able to explain how the image was made, or how it has been preserved.

This apparition, now nearly 500 years old, still inspires Catholics every day throughout the West, especially Mexicans and Mexican Americans. We keep the image of Our Lady of Guadalupe in our homes. We tell her story — the *Nican Mopohua* ("Here it is told"), written down in the Náhuatl language in 1556 — to our children and our children's children. We pray and speak to Our Lady as our spiritual mother. Every year, we celebrate her appearance with an all-night vigil of song and prayer that leads to a Mass celebrated at midnight on December 12, the day she gave her sign of roses.

When I was growing up in Monterrey, most summers my parents would take the family on the 600-mile journey to visit my grandparents in Mexico City. And every time we went, we would make a pilgrimage together as a family to the Basilica of Our Lady of Guadalupe. This is a normal thing to do for many Mexican families. I remember my father going on pilgrimage to the local shrine in Monterrey. All the men would do that around December 12. Company by company, factory by factory, they would walk for miles to the shrine to express their love for the Virgin.

I see this faith every day at the Cathedral of Our Lady of the Angels here in Los Angeles. We recently dedicated a chapel that contains a tiny and precious piece of the miraculous *tilma* — the only relic of its kind anywhere in the world outside of Mexico City. Our chapel has become a place of prayer and pilgrimage for individuals and families from all over the world.

And in these days, when our nation is struggling with its identity, struggling to find a place for millions of Mexicans who want to join us as Americans, I find myself in this chapel reflecting on the meaning of Our Lady of Guadalupe for the history of salvation and for America's future.

Following the apparition of Our Lady of Guadalupe, Mexico became the missionary base from which most of North

America and South America, and parts of Asia, were first evangelized. Within decades, Spanish missionaries from Mexico had spread the Christian faith — not only throughout Latin America and North America, but also into the Caribbean, the Philippines, and deeper into the countries of Asia and Oceania.

This is the beginning of the rest of the story of America's founding. A century before the Pilgrims arrived at Plymouth Rock, and long before the English settlement at Jamestown, the Hispanic Catholic presence was firmly established in America. Spanish priests traveling with Ponce de León near southeast Florida in 1521 celebrated the first Eucharist in the present boundaries of the United States. Catholics from Asia began arriving during this period, too, with the first Filipinos arriving at Morro Bay, California, in 1587 on a Spanish ship named for the Mother of Christ, *Nuestra Señora de la Esperanza* (*"Our Lady of Hope"*).

The first "Thanksgiving" was not celebrated by the Pilgrims in Plymouth, Massachusetts, in 1621. It was celebrated by Spanish missionary priests a half-century earlier in what is now Saint Augustine, Florida, in 1565.

Father López de Mendoza Grajales, one of four priests traveling with the pious Spanish explorer Pedro Menéndez de Avilés told the story of that first thanksgiving. Their expedition first spied land on the day the Church traditionally remembers the death of Saint Augustine, August 28. Following a series of skirmishes with French warships, Menéndez and his crew were eventually able to land two weeks later.

It was September 8, the date on which the Church celebrates the birth of the Blessed Virgin Mary. Father López said he and his brother priests came ashore and planted a large cross in the sand. Then all the crew marched up to the cross, knelt down before it, and kissed it. The whole time, they were singing an ancient hymn, *Te Deum* ("Thee, O God, We Praise").

While that was going on, a crowd of native people gathered on the beach and they began doing what they saw the missionaries doing — kneeling and kissing the cross themselves. After that, the priests celebrated a solemn Mass in honor of the Nativity of Mary. Then they all sat down together with the natives and ate a thanksgiving meal.

By the time of that first "thanksgiving," the Hispanic Catholic presence had already been established on the other side of the country, in the American Southwest, for at least twenty years. Within a decade of the apparition at Tepeyac, Juan Rodríguez Cabrillo had come up from Mexico and explored the California coast in a ship called San Salvador — "Holy Savior." He brought a priest with him, Fray Julián de Lescano, an Augustinian monk. Fray Julián probably celebrated the first holy Mass on California soil.

California was originally Mexican mission territory. Generations of missionaries came up from Mexico to spread the faith. The most famous was the great Franciscan priest Blessed Junípero Serra. He and his colleagues built mission churches up and down the long Pacific coastal road they called the King's Highway, *El Camino Real*.

Los Angeles was founded relatively late, in 1781. It was first called *El Pueblo de Nuestra Señora de los Ángeles* and was named after the little chapel in Italy that Saint Francis of Assisi used as his headquarters. The chapel was dedicated to the angels of God and the Mother of Jesus Christ, who is the queen of all the angels in heaven.

By that time, Hispanic immigrant missionaries had for centuries been naming this continent's rivers, mountains, and territories for saints, sacraments, and articles of the faith. We take these names for granted now — *Sacramento* ("Holy Sacrament"), *Las Cruces* ("Crosses"), *Corpus Christi* ("Body of Christ"), *Santa Fe* ("Holy Faith"), *San Francisco* ("Saint Francis"), even the *Sangre de Cristo Mountains*, named for the precious blood of Christ. Even our geography testifies that our nation was born from the encounter with the Christian missionaries.

These Hispanic missionaries from Mexico were the first giants of the American spirit.

People like the Franciscan Magin Catalá and the Jesuit Father Eusebio Kino who evangelized the Southwest and Northwest territories.

One of my favorite figures from the first evangelization of America is Venerable Antonio Margil, a Franciscan priest who left his homeland in Spain to come to Mexico in 1683. He told his mother he was coming here because "millions of souls [were] lost for want of priests to dispel the darkness of unbelief." People used to call him "the Flying Padre." He often traveled forty to fifty miles a day, walking barefoot. Fray Antonio had a truly continental sense of mission. He established churches in Texas and Louisiana, as well as in Costa Rica, Nicaragua, Guatemala, and Mexico.

These missionaries from Mexico built a new civilization in the Americas. They built roads and churches and homes. They introduced the principles and practices of agriculture, industry, education, and government. They were serious students of the indigenous cultures they found here; they became experts in local languages, customs, and beliefs. They composed some of this continent's first dictionaries, Bible translations, prayer books, and ethnographic studies. These missionaries were creative and innovative in the modes of popular culture — teaching Christian faith and morals through music, dance, drama, art, and architecture.

The missionaries defended the native peoples against the greed and political ambitions of the colonizers. Blessed Junípero Serra is credited with writing one of North America's first defenses of human rights. Three years before the Declaration of Independence, he insisted on new laws to protect the native peoples from exploitation by military governors, arguing that the natives had basic rights under God and the natural law.

Two centuries before America's War of Independence, these missionaries shed their blood and gave their lives for the love of God and this country. People like Dominican Father Luiz Cáncer de Barbastro, who was beaten to death in Florida in 1549, and Jesuit Father Pedro Martínez, martyred in Georgia in 1566.

The first American martyr was Father Juan de Padilla, a Franciscan killed on the plains of Kansas in 1542 in the vicinity of what is now the town of Herington. He traveled throughout the West with the explorer Francisco Vázquez de Coronado, and he is thought to be the first European to see the Grand Canyon.

Father de Padilla made many converts among the Quivira Indians. But when he and his companions went to a nearby village to evangelize a rival tribe, the Quivira ambushed and attacked them. Father de Padilla is said to have faced his execu-

tioners on his knees in prayer. As the historian Maryknoll Father
Albert Nevins said, it is fitting that the spot where Father de
Padilla was killed is "almost the geographical center" of what is
now the United States.

These are some of the missing pages in the story of
America's founding. Today, more than ever, we need to know this
heritage.

The nineteenth-century historian John Gilmary Shea said it
beautifully: "Mass was said to hallow the land and draw down
the blessing of heaven before the first step was taken to rear a
human habitation. The altar was older than the hearth." In other words, before any houses were built in America, they were
building altars. And those altars were built by Christian émigrés
from Mexico. Of course, before that still there were many tribes
of Native Americans who had their own distinctive tongues, cultures, and rituals of worship.

But what we need to keep in mind in our immigration debate
is that the Hispanic presence has deep roots in this soil. Long
before America had a name, long before there was a Washington,
D.C., or a Wall Street, this land was Spanish and Catholic. Two
hundred years before any of the Founding Fathers were born,
this land's people were being baptized in the name of Christ. The
people of this land were called Christians before they were called
Americans. And they were first called this name in the Spanish
tongue. Every American today, in some way, owes a spiritual debt

to these great Hispanic Catholic missionaries of the sixteenth and seventeenth centuries.

So why don't we know their stories? Because history is always told by the "winners." In America's case, the winners were the men who fought the American Revolution and established our national government. They handed down an American story, a national narrative that began with them and ignored earlier periods of American history.

They did this for a mix of reasons, but chiefly, perhaps, because they were unavoidably steeped in the anti-Catholic politics of post-Reformation Europe. Since Spanish and French Catholic missionaries made much of America's pre-colonial history, it was convenient for them to ignore it. Our current debates over immigration are still colored by prejudices that Philip Wayne Powell has called "Hispanophobia." Powell traces the roots of that attitude to the anti-Catholic "Black Legend" (*La Leyenda Negra*) — deeply negative folklore depicting Spaniards and their culture as depraved — spread by England beginning in the sixteenth century.

The history we have been told — the history of the winners — is not untrue. But it is biased and incomplete. And it is important today that we recognize that and correct it.

America needs a more accurate and honest story of its origins. We need a new understanding of the spiritual and religious motives at work in our nation's founding. We need a new appreciation of the ways our history intersects with the first evangelization of Mexico and the other lands of the Americas, *Nueva España*.

We need to tell the story of what the late University of

California historian Herbert Bolton used to call the "greater America." Bolton believed the only way to understand our nation was to consider our history in light of the "larger historical unities and interrelations of the Americas."

Then, as now, America's story is too often told without reference to the influence of other nations. Bolton put it bluntly:

> The study of thirteen English colonies and the
> United States in isolation has obscured many
> of the larger factors in their development, and
> helped to raise up a nation of chauvinists.

Written in the early 1930s, Bolton's words have a pointed meaning today as an America that has forgotten its beginnings wrestles with the growing presence of non-European and non-white immigrants and a future that is increasingly multicultural and multiracial.

So we need to understand "the greater America" — America in light of the Christian mission to the Americas, from the top of what is now Canada to the ends of South America and across to the Caribbean. America is actually the historical product of at least three very different Christian "missions" — the first missions of the Spanish and French Catholics and the later settlements of the Puritans from England.

Part of the mystery of our country is that it has always been a place for the encounter of every culture and people from all the ends of the earth. It's also the place where the main branches of European Christianity have met. Americans are both children of the Protestant Reformation that prevailed in England and children of the Catholic renewal, or Counter-Reformation, that was centered in Spain and Rome.

Especially now, when we face such divisive arguments over Mexican immigration, we need to appreciate the Spanish influence in our country and the Hispanic-Catholic mission to *all of the Americas.*

As Bolton warned, without the rest of the American story, we are left with a distorted idea of American identity and national culture. And at certain moments in American history, this incomplete sense of American identity has led to grave injustices. I am afraid we could be in one of those historical moments right now.

THREE

AMERICAN CREED

One of the country's great scholars of immigration, Oscar Handlin, was the son of Jewish immigrants who fled religious persecution in Russia. They came to Brooklyn, New York, by way of Ellis Island in the early years of the last century. Handlin won the Pulitzer Prize for history for his 1951 book, *The Uprooted,* which began with this bold statement: "Once I thought to write a history of the immigrants in America. Then I discovered that the immigrants *were* American history."

The history of America is still told as the story of immigration. And for good reason. From the beginning, the immigrant experience has been essential to America's self-identity.

Hector St. John de Crévecoer, a French émigré and farmer in upstate New York, was one of the first to try to define "what is an American." In a letter that dates to the years just after the American Revolution, he described how "in this great American asylum, the poor of Europe have by some means met together, and in consequence of various causes." Crévecoer had an almost religious fervor about the saving power of the American dream:

> Urged by a variety of motives, here they came.
> Everything has tended to regenerate them: new
> laws, a new mode of living, a new social system;
> here they are become men: in Europe they were
> as so many useless plants ... they withered
> and were mowed down by want, hunger, and
> war; but now, by the power of transplantation
> ... they have taken root and flourished. ...
> By what invisible power hath this surprising
> metamorphosis been performed? By that of
> the laws and that of their industry. The laws,
> the indulgent laws, protect them as they arrive,
> stamping on them the symbol of adoption; they
> receive ample rewards for their labors; these
> accumulated rewards procure them lands; those
> lands confer on them the title of freemen, and
> to that title every benefit is affixed which men
> can possibly require. This is the great operation
> daily performed by our laws.

This is one of the earliest and most heartfelt descriptions of the process of assimilation or Americanization. Crévecoer was also probably the first to speak of America as a *melting pot*. He imagined that upon coming to America immigrants' distinctive religious, political, and ethnic characteristics were being blended into a new national identity. "The American is a new man," he said. "Here individuals of all nations are melted into a new race of men, whose labors and posterity will one day cause great changes in the world."

But the process of assimilation and Americanization has never been easy. The famous poem at the base of the Statue of Liberty promises that America will be the "Mother of Exiles" who offers "worldwide welcome" through her "golden door." The reality of our history has been more complicated.

I think about that every time I travel to our nation's capital and see that other symbol of America, the Washington Monument. Visitors often notice that the monument changes colors about one-quarter of the way up from the ground. The marble at the monument's base is gray and white, but at a certain point the marble becomes brownish-white. Those differently colored stones tell another story about immigration and America.

Construction on the monument got underway in 1848. As a sign of national unity, the various states contributed stones for building the monument's interior walls. Foreign nations expressed their solidarity by sending marble and granite. In that spirit of friendship, Pope Pius IX sent a stone from the 2,000-year-old Temple of Concord in Rome.

What happened next can only be understood in the context of the anti-immigrant and anti-Catholic currents then stirring in the country. It is hard for us to remember that there was a time in America when Catholics were treated like second-class citizens. That was the case from the early days of the Republic. Harvard historian Arthur M. Schlesinger Sr. once said anti-Catholicism was "the deepest bias in the history of the American people."

Hatred of Catholicism was once so mainstream that books like

Six Months in a Convent, and *Awful Disclosures by Maria Monk of the Hotel Dieu Nunnery in Montreal* — fraudulent "exposés" — were bestsellers. Traveling carnival shows featured actors claiming to be ex-priests and ex-nuns telling sordid tales in lurid detail. Bigots burned down Catholic churches and convents. A priest in Maine was tarred and feathered. He later became the first president of Boston College, but the incident scarred him for life.

In this cultural context, an influential secret society and political party, the Order of the Star-Spangled Banner, popularly called the "Know-Nothings," started a rumor about the pope's gift to the Washington Monument. The Know-Nothings were pro-slavery, anti-immigrant, anti-Catholic and "nativist." They wanted to keep America "pure" and for "natives" only — which for them meant people of white, Anglo-European and Protestant descent.

The Know-Nothings feared the waves of new immigrants from Southern and Eastern Europe who began arriving in the 1820s and 1830s. They argued that these new immigrants came from inferior backgrounds; that they were lazy, uneducated, and inclined to criminal activity; that they wouldn't learn English; that they didn't share American values and weren't interested in becoming loyal citizens.

The Know-Nothings considered Catholics to be foreign agents of the pope. Nowadays their ideas might sound paranoid and imbalanced. But at the time the Washington Monument was being built, the Know-Nothings were a powerful political force. They held six governors' seats and seventy-five seats in Congress. Their candidate for president, former President Millard Fillmore, would win almost one-quarter of the popular vote in 1856.

The Know-Nothings exploited anti-immigrant and anti-Catholic fears. They convinced people that once the pope's stone was fitted into the Washington Monument, it would be the signal for the pope and his allies in lower Europe to invade and take over America. That was the context when, on March 6, 1854, just before dawn, a group of Know-Nothings came and stole the stone Pope Pius had sent.

Historians have never been able to determine what happened to it. Some believe it was smashed to pieces. Others think it was dumped into the nearby Potomac River. Whatever happened, the affair threw the monument project into chaos, funds dried up, the Civil War intervened, and it would be another thirty years before the monument was completed. By that time the builders were forced to use marble from a different quarry. And that is why we see the change of colors today.

It is fitting that this central symbol in our nation's capital bears a visible scar of America's long and continuing struggle with questions of race, religion, and immigration.

The Washington Monument should remind us that while America has been generous and welcoming of immigrants, we have also been a nation that at times throughout its history has been bitterly divided along racial, ethnic, and even religious lines. The monument should remind us that America has also been a nation where indigenous peoples were driven from their lands, where blacks were lynched, Japanese-Americans were jailed in collective punishment, and where laws and public opinion have supported slavery, racial segregation, eugenic experimentation on the "unfit," and the exclusion of immigrants on the basis of race and country of origin.

These are inconvenient, unflattering memories. But as we debate immigration today, we need to remember that our nation has always been troubled and conflicted on questions of race and immigration, and often religion.

In his last book, *Where Do We Go From Here* (1967), Rev. Martin Luther King Jr. said: "Ever since the birth of our nation, white America has had a schizophrenic personality on the question of race. She has been torn between selves — a self in which she proudly professed the great principles of democracy and a self in which she sadly practiced the antithesis of democracy."

What King says is true as a matter of historical fact. The story of American immigration usually doesn't include the millions who were violently "emigrated" to this country against their will — the men, women, and children forced to come to this country in chains from Africa and elsewhere. But it should. Because the question of race in America runs deeper than black and white, and deeper than our nation's "original sin" of slavery.

Race has always been central to American immigration policy and our attitudes about immigrants. This is still true. Immigration is tied to the larger question of "What is an American?" — to our idea of what this country is meant to be, and what it means to belong to this country. Sadly, the answers that many Americans give to those questions reflect a deep-seated racial bias.

I don't believe America's dark chapters of prejudice reflect who we really are as a people or as a nation. But we need to confront these dark chapters to remind us of who we are prone to become if we are not careful in our thinking and in our words and actions.

The common thread of prejudice we find throughout American history is the desire to define "who is an American" along narrow racial, ethnic, and religious grounds. Abraham Lincoln warned of this disturbing pattern in our civic life in a pessimistic letter he wrote in August 1855, about a year after the Washington Monument incident.

> Our progress in degeneracy appears to me to be pretty rapid. As a nation, we began by declaring that "all men are created equal." We now practically read it "all men are created equal, except Negroes." When the Know-Nothings get control, it will read "all men are created equal, except Negroes, and foreigners, and Catholics."

Lincoln points us to the basic irony of American history, as King would a century later. The irony is the persistent conflict between our founding principles and our political actions and attitudes, the conflict between the ideals of America and the reality.

America remains unique among the family of nations. Other nations have been established on the basis of a common territory or a common race, ethnicity or religion — on the ties of land or kinship or faith. America is built instead on the foundation of an ideal, a vision, a dream.

G. K. Chesterton said famously, "America is the only nation in the world that is founded on a creed."

It has always interested me that outsiders have written some of the most penetrating commentaries on America. The greatest, of course, is *Democracy in America,* written in the 1830s by a French Catholic, Alexis de Tocqueville. But in some ways, I find Chesterton's *What I Saw in America* (1922) more insightful and even prophetic about our current realities.

Writing as a British Catholic, Chesterton found America's "creed" expressed "with dogmatic and even theological lucidity" in the first lines of our Declaration of Independence.

> We hold these truths to be self-evident, that all
> men are created equal, that they are endowed
> by their Creator with certain unalienable
> Rights, that among these are Life, Liberty and
> the pursuit of Happiness. That, to secure these
> rights, governments are instituted among men,
> deriving their just powers from the consent of
> the governed …

The American creed, as Chesterton and many others have recognized, is rooted in the Jewish and Christian Scriptures and the culture and thought-world created by those traditions. Rev. Dietrich Bonhoeffer, the German Lutheran martyred at the hands of the Nazis, taught for a time in New York City in the

1930s. In his *Ethics,* he later wrote about the Christian spirit he found in America's national charter.

> American democracy is not founded upon
> the emancipated man but quite the contrary,
> upon the kingdom of God and the limitation
> of earthly powers by the sovereignty of God.
> ... The federal Constitution was written by
> men who were conscious of original sin and
> of the wickedness of the human heart. Earthly
> wielders of power, and also the people, are
> directed into their proper bounds, in due
> consideration of man's innate longing for power
> and of the fact that Power pertains only to God.

The men who wrote America's Declaration of Independence and federal Constitution were not all orthodox Christians. They were men of the Enlightenment who were proud to rely more on reason than on faith. Many of them were, in fact, Deists. Nonetheless, they gave us a political philosophy and a system of law and government that reflects the Jewish and Christian understanding of God, nature, and the human person. As the French Catholic philosopher Jacques Maritain observed in his *Reflections on America* (1958):

> Far beyond the influences received either
> from Locke or the eighteenth-century
> Enlightenment, the American Constitution
> ... is deep-rooted in the age-old heritage of

Christian thought and civilization. ... The founding fathers were neither metaphysicians nor theologians, but their philosophy of life and their political philosophy, their notion of natural law and of human rights, were permeated with concepts worked out by Christian reason and backed up by an unshakeable religious feeling.

The American creed reflects both the Christian humanism of America's political founders and the redemptive motives that impelled the first missionaries more than a century before our founding documents were written.

We need to remember that America's founding documents do more than set forth principles and procedures to give order to our common life together. Like all creeds, our founding documents define the identity of those who "believe" in them. These documents reflect a set of assumptions about human life — about who we are, about our destiny, and about how we should live our lives. This understanding is the heart of what we might call the American spirit. This understanding is the answer to the question, "What is an American?" Or it should be.

If we want to know what it means to be an American — and we must if we are going to meet the challenge of immigration in our day — then we need to reflect on the essentially religious vision that America's founders intended for this country. We need to know the articles of the American creed.

The fact is that our democracy and national identity are built on the pillars of four essentially religious assumptions. The first assumption is the sovereignty of God, who is the Lord of nations, peoples, and history. In the language of the Declaration of Independence, the American system is founded on a belief that the world is governed by "the Laws of Nature and of Nature's God," who is the "Supreme Judge of the World."

The second religious assumption that underlies America's national identity and institutions is the belief that all men and women have a divine beginning and a transcendent destiny. They are "created" *by* God and *for* God's purposes. The third assumption follows from the second: the God who created us also "endows" us with rights and freedoms so that we can fulfill his purposes for our lives.

In the Founders' religious vision, human rights and freedoms are universal — they do not depend on where one is born, or what racial or ethnic group one is born into. These rights and freedoms are also "unalienable." In those stirring words from President Kennedy's inaugural address, "The rights of man come not from the generosity of the state but from the hand of God." It follows that what comes from God's hands can never be denied or taken away by any government of men.

The fourth and final religious assumption that underlies American democracy is the belief that government exists to secure justice, which is defined as the promotion and protection of these God-given "unalienable" rights. In fact, for America's founders, government has no other purpose than to secure these rights — broadly defined as the rights to life, liberty, and the pursuit of happiness.

It is seldom talked about today, even in our history books, but some of America's founders believed strongly that the essential liberties given by God include the natural right to immigration. In a pamphlet he wrote in 1774, Thomas Jefferson said that our natural human freedom demands that we have

> a right, which nature has given to all men, of departing from the country in which chance, not choice has placed them, of going in quest of new habitations, and of there establishing new societies, under such laws and regulations as to them shall seem most likely to promote public happiness.

It should be added that, in practice, Jefferson and his fellow founders struggled between this universalist vision of immigration and their own racial bias toward the superiority of white Anglo-Saxons. But they left us a Declaration of Independence that forever calls America to "the naturalization of foreigners" and "to encourage their migrations."

America's founders also believed that freedom of conscience and the right to religious liberty were endowed by God and must be promoted and protected by our government. They went further than that — they held that democracy depends on having a moral and virtuous population. And they knew the best guarantee for that is a civil society in which individuals and religious institutions were free to live, act, and vote according to their values and principles.

As John Adams put it famously in a message to the Massachusetts militia in 1798: "Our Constitution was made only for a moral and religious people. It is wholly inadequate to the government of any other."

The American creed reflects the amazing universalism of the Christian Gospel and the later prophets of Israel. This creed has helped make our country home to a flourishing diversity of cultures, religions, and ways of life. As a result, we have always been a nation of nationalities. *E pluribus unum.* One people made from peoples of many nations, races, and creeds.

For sure, there were moral blind spots in the Founders' vision of how this creed should be interpreted; the Constitution they drafted denies full rights to slaves and women. And as commentators from Abraham Lincoln to Martin Luther King Jr. have observed, throughout our history we have faced the persistent challenge of living up to our ideals.

This is the challenge we now face in our immigration debate. This challenge requires that we examine our conscience about our commitment to the American creed. It also requires that we take a hard look at our attitudes about race and our assumptions about what it means to be an American. Because as we see throughout our history, in times of fear and uncertainty, we have often been tempted to abandon our commitment to liberty and justice for all in favor of an insular, racial definition of who can be a true American.

This temptation has contributed to those moments in our history that we are the least proud of — slavery and segregation; the treatment of Native Americans; periodic outbreaks of nativism, anti-Catholicism, and anti-Semitism; the internment of Japanese-Americans during World War II; the rise of white supremacist ideology and groups like the Ku Klux Klan; the eugenics experiments of the 1920s; the misadventures caused by the ideology of "manifest destiny" — the sense that God is on our side as his chosen people and "redeemer nation."

These dark moments in our history reflect a basic tension in our national soul. Do we really believe that America is one nation under God, made up from every other people? Or is America instead a nation that is essentially white, Anglo-Saxon, and Protestant, but *permits* the presence of peoples of other races, colors, and religions?

This tension has been reflected in our immigration policy from the beginning. America's first naturalization law, passed in 1790, limited citizenship to immigrants who were "free white persons." Even from the start, civic leaders assumed America's "melting pot" was meant for white Europeans only. Over the years, many of our ideas about who is a true American have unfortunately been shaped by a founding belief that the white race is superior to all others.

In the late nineteenth century, paranoia about a "Yellow Peril" — that "Orientals" were overrunning the country — led Congress to pass a series of laws that banned Asians from emigrating or becoming citizens. In 1924, Congress established a quota system to block Japanese, Chinese, and Filipino immigration. At the same time, Congress blocked Jewish immigration from Poland and Russia and immigration from India and the Middle East. This racial quota system remained in place until the comprehensive immigration reform legislation of 1965.

The motive behind these policies was that "America must be kept American." That's how President Calvin Coolidge explained it in 1923. But the idea of America reflected in these policies was never worthy of America's founders — because it was based on an idea of America that was not true to the creed they gave us.

We face a similar dilemma today. Fears about America's future have given rise to a new nativism. The arguments of today's nativists aren't much different than those of nativists in years gone by. Their idea is that "real" Americans descend from white Europeans and that our culture is based on the individualism, work ethic, and rule of law that we inherited from our Anglo-Protestant forebears.

The intellectual and political justification for the new nativism was set out a few years ago in *Who Are We?* (2005), a highly influential book written by the late Samuel Huntington of Harvard. Huntington was a wise student of American life and the world order. He wrote always from a sincere love for this country. But in my opinion, in his final book he let his anxieties about America's future get the best of him.

Who Are We? is the product of more than a decade of speeches and articles in which Huntington issued a kind of increasingly anxious call to arms — to defend America against what he described as a literal invasion of immigrants, especially Mexicans. In his words:

Mexican immigration is a unique, disturbing,
and looming challenge to our cultural integrity,
our national identity, and potentially to our
future as a country.

Demographically, socially, and culturally, the
Reconquista (reconquest) of the Southwest
United States by Mexican immigrants is well
underway.

In the face of this demographic "threat," Huntington proposed his own version of what he called the "American Creed."
For him, the Founders' creed was not a commitment to an essentially religious vision of humanity and government. Instead,
America's creed is a set of propositions that emerge from an exclusively European cultural background.

The Creed ... was the product of the distinct
Anglo-Protestant culture of the founding
settlers of America in the seventeenth and
eighteenth centuries. Key elements of that
culture include: the English language;
Christianity; religious commitment; English
concepts of the rule of law, the responsibility
of rulers, and the rights of individuals; and
dissenting Protestant values of individualism,
the work ethic, and the belief that humans have
the ability and the duty to try to create a heaven
on earth, a "city on the hill."

Huntington insisted he was not claiming that America is an Anglo-Protestant country. But it sure sounded like he was. He argued that Mexicans were a threat to our American identity and way of life precisely because there are "profound differences" between their culture and America's Anglo-Protestant culture. According to Huntington, Mexican traditions and values are rooted in a "culture of Catholicism" — a culture that he said can never be reconciled with the American creed.

Huntington presented a catalog of anti-Catholic and anti-Mexican stereotypes. He seemed to be deliberate in making sure that he was always quoting someone else, usually a Latino, to make his case. But his intent seems unmistakable — to "prove" that Mexicans' values keep them poor, uneducated, unable to learn English, and unfit to be welcomed in America.

Mexicans, he argued, suffer from the "*mañana* syndrome" — they don't care about the quality of the work they do, or getting it done on time. Their attitude is "Who cares? That is good enough," he said. Huntington quoted for evidence one Latino who claimed he didn't know anyone in his Mexican neighborhood who believed in "education and hard work."

Huntington quoted another who said that Mexicans will never succeed in America because they have a "mistrust of people outside the family; lack of initiative, self-reliance, and ambition; low priority for education; acceptance of poverty as a virtue necessary for entrance into heaven."

Those of us who are Mexican might respond to this kind of intellectual bigotry by pointing to the proud legacy of Mexican and Latin American literature, art, and architecture, and to the great achievements of Spanish theology and spirituality. Or we could talk about the Mexicans we know who are the tops in their fields in business, government, medicine, and culture.

We could also point out that Huntington's anti-Mexican stereotypes have all been deployed before — by the Know-Nothings and other nativist groups — to describe earlier generations of immigrants. Whether it's Mexicans, Irish, Italians, Germans, Hungarians, Chinese, Jews, or Poles, it's always the same set of libels — they are inferior people; they don't work hard; they aren't smart enough; they won't learn our language; they're loyal to their own country; and they resent our laws and traditions.

I would never deny that Mexican and Hispanic culture are different. A continental European perspective shapes the Hispanic sense of law and government, which is definitely different from the Anglo-Saxon ideas of America's founders. There is also a different "sense of life" that comes from Hispanic culture.

But Huntington would have us see these cultural differences as evidence of cultural deficiency and inferiority. In this, he makes the mistake we have seen too often in American history — the mistake of assuming European white racial superiority. Sad to say that in our immigration debates today, we often hear ideas like Huntington's being repeated on cable television, talk radio, and Internet blogs, and even by some of our political leaders.

Huntington is right that English Protestants gave us our basic institutions and assumptions about government, work, and the common law. We should celebrate the Anglo-Protestant men and women who helped shape our civic culture and moral worldview, and we should deepen our commitment to their ideals and traditions. But the laws, culture, and traditions that our Anglo-Protestant founders gave us aren't meant to *exclude* and *divide*. They are meant to *include* and *unite*. This is the genius of America. Our institutions and traditions are universal, they aren't determined by any one culture. They are based on God's sovereignty and the equality of the human person.

That is what Chesterton saw in America. That's what he described as "the great American experiment, the experiment of a democracy of diverse races." For Chesterton, what makes America unique — even revolutionary — is our expansive and inclusive ideal of citizenship: "America invites all men to become citizens; but it implies the dogma that there is such a thing as citizenship."

What Chesterton calls our "dogma" of citizenship is based on the Founders' belief in "the divine origin of man" and the "fact that God created all men equal." The nativist impulse is to deny this dogma. The nativist presumes that those who came to this country earlier are somehow superior or "more equal" than those who came after and those who are still coming. Citizenship, for them, is not open to all men and women. It is reserved for those who fit certain economic and racial categories.

Nativism is a heresy, a perversion of the American creed. Only those descended from the tribes that greeted the first missionaries have any claim to being called "natives." The rest of us are immigrants or the children of immigrants. There is no one who is unworthy to be welcomed as our fellow citizen.

This is not who we are as Americans. We are not nativists, we are not racists, and we are not xenophobes. But our history teaches that when we get scared, we want to close ranks and close the "golden door" of America to foreigners. In today's immigration debate we need to be honest with ourselves. We must acknowledge that there have been times in our history when we have allowed our fears to drag us down, and caused us to forget our creed and our national identity. We cannot let this become one of those times. Our task today is to confront our fears and resist the temptations to narrow the horizons of who can be an American.

So we need to tell a new story about ourselves and about America — a new story that includes the mission to the New World, the story of the "greater America." The story of how this country was formed from the blood and sacrifice and faith of many peoples.

We also need to make a new commitment to the American creed, as the first missionaries and the Founding Fathers alike taught it. We need to have the courage to honor and carry on their vision. We need to believe what they believed — that we are all children of the same God, and that God does not make some of his children from inferior, less worthy stock.

FOUR

CATHOLICS IN AMERICA

The Catholic vision of America has been deeply marked by our experience as an immigrant Church — and by more than a century of nativist hostility. Anti-Catholicism was institutionalized in America from the beginning. Most of the original thirteen colonies barred Catholics from holding political office. Virginia and Massachusetts banned Catholics from even settling within their borders.

In the early 1800s, America's founding prejudice against Catholics was merged with anti-immigrant bias as waves of Catholics began pouring in from Ireland, Germany, and elsewhere. The backlash from America's Protestant and English elite along the Atlantic seaboard was harsh. Old religious bigotries mixed with new fears that American civilization was being overrun by hordes of poor, depraved, and backward peoples.

The nation's most respected Protestant preachers took to their pulpits and to the newspapers to warn that Catholic immigrants were enemies of democracy and would never make trustworthy neighbors or loyal citizens. Rev. Horace Bushnell warned: "Our first danger is barbarism; Romanism next."

In his influential book *Our Country* (1885), Rev. Josiah Strong also compared the newcomers to the barbarians who contributed to the fall of the Roman Empire. He warned that Catholic immigration was a threat not only to America's future, but also to the supremacy of the "Anglo-Saxon race":

> During the last four years we have suffered a peaceful invasion by an army, more than twice as vast as the estimated number of Goths and Vandals that swept over Southern Europe and overwhelmed Rome.

There is, of course, an irony to all these expressions of fear and hate. As we've seen, Catholics were in this land long before Protestants — beginning in the early sixteenth century when the first missionaries came from Spain by way of Mexico. When America's first president was still a toddler, Catholics were already operating charities, schools, hospitals, and orphanages to serve America's poor, a population that was mostly non-Catholic.

Today, Catholics make up America's largest faith community and there are Catholics serving on the U.S. Supreme Court, in Congress, and in the highest branches of the military and federal government. Across the country, there are Catholic governors and mayors, and Catholics serving in every state legislature and municipal government. The long years of institutional discrimination are forgotten now, although new, more deceptive forms of anti-Catholicism are emerging as our society grows more secularized and "de-Christianized."

Nonetheless, the Catholic Church continues to play a leading role in the nation's civic life — through our parishes, charities, social services, schools, and universities. As it has been since before the Republic was founded, the Catholic Church remains a profound force for human dignity and social justice in our communities. On immigration, the Church has always been a leader among America's faith communities — advocating for justice for immigrants and refugees, and giving material and spiritual support to those in our midst.

I believe our heritage as American Catholics gives us special responsibilities in today's debates over immigration reform. Many of us have forgotten our immigrant roots, but our Church remains a Church of immigrants. In earlier generations, we welcomed newcomers from every nation in Europe. Today, we are still welcoming newcomers — but they come now mainly from Latin America, Asia, Oceania, and Africa. We see this vividly here in Los Angeles where we count peoples from nearly sixty ethnicities, nationalities, and countries of origin. We see similar patterns in Catholic communities throughout the United States.

Because we are an immigrant Church, this debate over immigration is a debate about the future of the Church and our Catholic people. The Mexicans and Latin Americans at the center of the controversy — the millions whose fate is being decided by our politicians — are mostly fellow Catholics.

So we have a moral obligation, as Catholics and as citizens, to contribute to these discussions over immigration reform. The challenge we face is to remember who we are and where we came from. We need to testify to our history as Catholics in America — to the memory of our ancestors' experience of injustice and discrimination. We need to bring to the table our rich Catholic tradition of teaching on human dignity and social justice.

We also need to keep in mind that our faith requires that we address issues — not as Democrats or Republicans, or as conservatives or liberals — but as believers who are aware that we are accountable to God. As always, the best service Catholics can offer to our country as citizens is to make political judgments and actions that are rooted in our religious convictions and moral values.

Catholic social doctrine has much to offer American society on many levels. When I say this, I want to make something clear. Catholics have no desire to impose our views on our neighbors. Our social doctrine is not sectarian but universal. The Church's teaching reflects the natural law that God has placed in the heart of every man and woman — the same natural law that America's founders cited as a foundation for our experiment in democracy.

The basic principles of Catholic teaching are consistent with American values and are shared by our neighbors of other faiths, and even by those who don't profess any faith. Our principles lead us to seek justice and the common good, to defend the innocent and lift up the weak, and to promote the freedom and dignity of the human person. When it comes to solving social problems, we believe in *subsidiarity* — the principle that the more local and small-scale the solutions, the better.

The Catholic Church's interest in immigration reform today doesn't grow out of any political or partisan agenda. It is rooted in our religious identity and faith commitments as Catholics.

The Church exists for only one purpose — to carry out the mission that Jesus Christ gave to her in Jerusalem 2,000 years ago. Jesus commanded his Church to proclaim God's kingdom and his Gospel of life to every nation. So, by definition, the Church's mission transcends boundaries of race, culture, and nation. *Catholic* means *universal*, in the sense of wholeness and totality. The Church's calling is global.

Catholics believe we are working with God to help create — from out of the world's many peoples — one single family of God. In the New Testament, the Church's mission is revealed at Pentecost, fifty days after Jesus' resurrection. The story goes that on that day, devout men and women had gathered in Jerusalem "from every nation under heaven." The scene in the second chapter of the Acts of the Apostles lists a dozen national and ethnic groups, a list meant to represent the whole known world and all its peoples:

> Parthians and Medes and Elamites and
> residents of Mesopotamia, Judea and
> Cappadocia. Pontus and Asia, Phrygia and
> Pamphylia, Egypt and the parts of Libya
> belonging to Cyrene, and visitors from

Rome, both Jews and proselytes, Cretans and
Arabians.

Everyone present at that first Pentecost heard the apostles'
preaching "each ... in his own language." That's still the Catholic
mission — to proclaim God to everyone who dwells on the face of
earth. The Bible's last book, Revelation, sees this mission fulfilled
in a new world where a vast multitude is assembled "from every
nation, from all tribes and peoples and tongues."

Jesus said his kingdom was not of this world. But the Church
carries out her mission *in* this world — on earth and in history. As Jesus did, Catholics walk with the people we are called to
serve in every time and in every place. As Jesus did, we share
their hopes and joys, their worries and their sufferings.

Through the centuries, our mission has brought us into con-
tact with every type of cultural reality, government system, and
economic order. And the Church has gained a lot of insight into
human behavior and society. The Gospel says that Jesus didn't
need anyone to tell him anything about human nature — "for
he himself knew what was in man." We can say the same thing
about the Church. Pope Paul VI once called the Catholic Church
an "expert in humanity." I think that's true.

The Church has developed a rich body of teachings on questions related to society, government, economics, and international relations. Our social doctrine is not an ideology or political
platform. It's not a set of technical solutions. The Church presents
moral principles and rational analysis to help people evaluate social conditions so they can take actions in light of the Gospel's
demands of justice and love.

The Church's immigration teachings form a small part of this larger body of Catholic social doctrine. These teachings grow out of our reflections on the Bible and also out of our practical experience of caring for pilgrims, refugees, exiles, and migrants.

Catholic commitments to the immigrant also have deeper, more personal roots. Our commitments form a part of our original identity as believers. Put simply, we care for the immigrant because Jesus commanded us to. Catholics must defend immigrants if we are going to be worthy of the name Christian.

Other cultures and religions have traditions of welcoming the stranger. Ancient philosophers like Plato wrote about the importance of hospitality. But in Christianity, care for the stranger becomes a sacred obligation, a personal duty. This duty is rooted in early Christianity's Jewish heritage.

Strangers sojourning in foreign lands have always been a vulnerable class of people. The Jewish people experienced this firsthand. They were enslaved and exploited while living as migrants in Egypt some 2,000 years before the Christian era. The Jews emerged from that experience to become the first people to include love for the immigrant and sojourner as one of their religious and ethical duties. The Jewish Scriptures are filled with commands to treat immigrants with compassion and justice. Moses, speaking in the name of God, reminded them:

You shall not oppress a stranger; you know the

heart of a stranger, for you were strangers in the
land of Egypt.

In his early life, Jesus Christ relived the experiences of Moses
and the people of Israel. The Gospel of Matthew tells us that
shortly after Jesus was born, his family was forced into exile in
Egypt by the persecution of King Herod. Like his Jewish ancestors, Jesus was to know what it felt like to be driven out by political or economic need, to become a refugee and an immigrant, a
stranger in a strange land.

Years later, when Jesus talked about God's final judgment on
our souls, he identified himself with the poor and vulnerable —
and specifically with the "stranger." In Jesus' ethics, our love for
God can never be separated from our love for our neighbor. And
he told us that we must look for him — for the image of God — in
the least of our brothers and sisters.

God will judge each of us according to whether we "welcome"
him in the stranger, Jesus said. For those who refuse to see God's
image in the immigrant, he holds out little hope:

Then [God] will say ... "Depart from me, you
cursed, into the eternal fire. ... I was a stranger
and you did not welcome me."

Hospitality — literally the "love of strangers" — became a basic virtue for Jesus' followers. To be a Christian was to practice
hospitality toward the stranger. We see this teaching already in
the New Testament. The Letter to the Hebrews commands, "Do
not neglect to show hospitality to strangers, for thereby some

have entertained angels unawares." This refers to the story in the Jewish Scriptures of how God appeared to the patriarch Abraham in the form of three strangers.

The demands of hospitality and welcoming the stranger are not easy to carry out today — and they weren't easy for the first Christians to carry out either. We find evidence of this also in the New Testament. In his first letter, Saint Peter had to urge his people to "practice hospitality *ungrudgingly.*"

His word choice here tells us a lot about how seriously the early Church considered the duty of hospitality. The word he used is actually the Greek word "murmuring" (*gongyzō*), which was first used in the story of the Jewish people's forty years of wandering in the wilderness after their liberation from Egypt. During that journey, at different points along the way, the people got frustrated and "murmured" or complained against Moses and God. This was a pivotal point in Jewish history, a test of faith. And throughout their Scriptures, the moment was remembered; the word "murmuring" came to be applied to those who are too stubborn or hardhearted to have faith in God or to follow his teachings.

In this tradition, Peter is saying — then and now — that Christians who "murmur" about the strangers in their midst show that they lack love and faith in God's promises and commands.

Jesus' teaching became the foundation for Christian ethics and the motive for the Church's ministries and advocacy for migrants and refugees. Jesus was remembered as one who chose to live as an immigrant. Saint Gregory of Nazianzen referred to him as "Christ, who for your sake was a stranger."

The first Christians understood his parable of the last judgment literally. Saint Jerome instructed his disciples: "Let poor men and strangers be acquainted with your modest table, and with them Christ shall be your guest."

They believed he was truly present in the poor and the immigrant — just as he was truly present in the consecrated bread and wine of the Eucharist. Saint John Chrysostom said:

> Do you wish to honor the body of Christ? …
> Do not pay him homage in the temple clad in
> silk, only then to neglect him outside where
> he suffers cold and nakedness. He who said:
> "This is my body" is the same one who said …
> "Whatever you did to the least of my brothers
> you did also to me."

John Chrysostom was Archbishop of Constantinople in the late fourth century. He cared for at least 3,000 poor people, including many who were strangers, refugees, and pilgrims "absent from their home." He and other Church leaders began setting up lodgings they called *xenodochia* (literally, "a place for receiving strangers"). These lodgings are the origins for our modern charities and hospitals.

The Church's outreach to immigrants was not always popular with local governments and political officials. In a letter that survives from the year 374, we hear Saint Basil defending his work to an angry provincial governor named Elias in Cappadocia (modern-day Turkey).

> And whom do we wrong by building inns
> for guests, both those visiting us on their
> journey and those needing some treatment in
> their illness, and by appointing for them the
> necessary comforts — nurses, doctors, beasts of
> burden, and [priests]?

Until the coming of Christianity, there were no organized social services and no ethic of responsibility for the poor. Christians distinguished themselves by their love for the poor and sick, as the Christian leader Tertullian wrote in the late second century.

> It is our care of the helpless, our practice of
> loving kindness, that brands us in the eyes of
> many of our opponents. "Only look," they say,
> "look how they love one another!"

One of the Church's chief opponents was the ex-Catholic Emperor Julian, known as Julian the Apostate. Julian used his bully pulpit as emperor to scorn Christianity and promote devotion to Greek and Roman deities. But he never could get over how the Christians loved one another and how they sacrificed to serve the poor. In 362, he wrote a letter urging Romans to follow the Christian example and establish their own charities. What's interesting is that Julian singled out only one area of Christian charity — what he called "their benevolence to strangers," including the immigrants among them.

From the beginning, to be Christian was to be identified with this benevolence to strangers. In a sermon delivered near the end of the Roman Empire, Saint Augustine gave advice that could stand as a summary of our Christian obligations then — and now:

> Be meek, sympathize with the suffering, carry
> the weak. *And in this time of so many strangers,*
> needy, and suffering people, *let your hospitality*
> *and good works abound.*

Care for the spiritual and material well-being of migrants is a practical duty for a global Church. As the Catholic faith spread throughout the world, bishops began establishing "national parishes" to serve foreigners living within their borders. This has been a distinctive feature of the Catholic Church in America, where we have long-standing national parishes for Poles, Germans, Italians, and others. Today, everywhere throughout the world, the Church follows the basic policy set out by the Fourth Lateran Council in 1215:

> We find in most countries, cities and dioceses
> … people of diverse languages who, though
> bound by one faith, have varied rites and
> customs. Therefore, we strictly enjoin that the
> bishops of these cities or dioceses provide the
> proper men who will celebrate the liturgical

functions according to their rites and languages [and] ... administer the sacraments of the Church and instruct their people by word and by deed.

Modern Catholic thinking on immigration is shaped by the experience of the massive waves of European emigration that started in the middle years of the nineteenth century. Many innovative agencies and initiatives were created during this period. This was also the time of the Church's great patron saints of immigration — John the Baptist Scalabrini, Vincent Pallotti, and Frances Xavier Cabrini, the Italian immigrant who was the first American citizen to become a canonized saint of the Catholic Church.

Catholic thinking today is also shaped by the Church's relief work in the various refugee crises of the twentieth century — the Spanish Civil War, the Mexican Revolution, World War I, World War II, and the 1948 war in Palestine. Pope Pius XII, who was head of the Church during these crisis years, was among the first world leaders to identify forced migration and population dislocations as a threat to human rights and international stability in the postwar world.

Pope Pius wrote the only papal document on immigration, 1952's *Exsul Familia Nazarethana* ("The Émigré Family of Nazareth"). Continuing the tradition of reflection that dates back to the early Church, Pope Pius begins by recalling that Jesus chose to share the humiliations and hardships of the world's millions of immigrants and refugees.

> The émigré Holy Family of Nazareth, fleeing
> into Egypt, is the archetype of every refugee
> family. Jesus, Mary and Joseph, living in exile
> in Egypt to escape the fury of an evil king, are,
> for all times and all places, the models and
> protectors of every migrant, alien, and refugee
> of whatever kind who, whether compelled by
> fear of persecution or by want, is forced to
> leave his native land, his beloved parents and
> relatives, his close friends, and to seek a foreign
> soil.

> For the almighty and most merciful God
> decreed that his only Son, "being made like
> unto men and appearing in the form of a man,"
> should, together with his Immaculate Virgin
> Mother and his holy guardian Joseph, be in this
> type too of hardship and grief, the firstborn
> among many brethren, and precede them in it.

Sixty years later, *Exsul Familia Nazarethana* remains vital for understanding the challenge of global migration. It is also striking to read the document's footnotes and to notice how often Pope Pius spoke to American leaders about this issue. Indeed, the pope's most important statements of Catholic principle were made to American audiences.

America has always intrigued the popes — for our territory that spans an entire continent; for our founders' inspiring vision of human liberty; for our prosperity and generosity; and for our heritage of welcoming immigrants and refugees. Pope Pius XII hoped that America would emerge as a model for charity and solidarity in the postwar world. But he was also aware that America was prone to sharp anti-immigrant backlashes.

In 1948, addressing a delegation of American congressmen studying the refugee situation in postwar Europe, he made a gentle appeal to their consciences:

> We dare say the further question has risen more
> than once in your minds, if not to your lips:
> is the present [American] immigration policy
> as liberal as the natural resources permit in a
> country so lavishly blessed by the Creator and
> as the challenging needs of other countries
> would seem to demand? Your travels will afford
> much data for the answer to that question.

On Christmas Eve of that same year, he wrote a letter to America's bishops that shows how attentive he was to American immigration policy.

> You know . . . with what anxiety we have
> followed those who have been forced by
> revolutions in their own countries, or by
> unemployment or hunger, to leave their homes
> and live in foreign lands.

The natural law itself, no less than devotion to humanity, urges that ways of migration be opened to these people. For the Creator of the universe made all good things primarily for the good of all.

Since land everywhere offers the possibility of supporting a large number of people, the sovereignty of the state, although it must be respected, cannot be exaggerated to the point that access to this land is, for inadequate and unjustified reasons, denied to needy and decent people from other nations, provided of course, that the public wealth, considered very carefully, does not forbid this.

Informed of our intentions, you recently strove for legislation to allow many refugees to enter your land. Through your persistence, a provident law was enacted, a law that we hope will be followed by others of broader scope. In addition, you have, with the aid of chosen men, cared for the emigrants as they left their homes and as they arrived in your land, thus admirably putting into practice the precept of priestly charity: "The priest is to injure no one; he will desire rather to aid all."

In this short passage, which he quotes in *Exsul Familia Nazarathena*, Pope Pius gives us a kind of compendium of the Church's social doctrine on immigration. This doctrine is rooted in the vision of human society that was taught by Jesus Christ. The Church believes that every person is created in God's image, and that society's purpose is to promote human dignity and the sanctity of the family.

Because everyone is a child of God, Catholics believe that human rights are not a privilege or license granted by governments or any other group. Human rights are "natural rights." That means these rights are *universal* and *unalienable*. These rights aren't contingent on whether you are a man or a woman, or on where you are born, or on what your racial or ethnic background is. These rights don't depend on the whims of politicians or other powerful interests; they don't depend on economic fortune or political circumstance.

For Catholics, human rights come from God. And what God has given, no one — no man, no institution, no legislature or court — can ever justify denying. These rights include the right to life, the most fundamental right, and the right to the things necessary to lead a life worthy of one's God-given dignity.

The natural right to immigration flows from the basic human right to life. In Catholic teaching, if you and your family are unable to secure life's necessities in your home country — due to political instability, economic distress, religious persecution, or other conditions that offend basic dignity — you must be free to seek these things in another country. That does not mean that we have an absolute right to live wherever we want whenever we want. But in a world divided by war, famine, persecution, and chronic economic dislocations, the right to immigration becomes a crucial guarantee of our rights to life, liberty, and the pursuit of happiness.

In Catholic teaching, this right to immigration also flows from our basic belief that God is the world's Creator and the Lord of history. Although we all have different ethnic origins and are spread across different continents, regions, and nations, we are all created by God to live as one family.

God created the good things of this earth — its natural resources and opportunities — for the benefit of everyone. These good things aren't meant only for a privileged few. Or only for people in certain countries. God intends the good things of his creation to be shared by all, no matter where we are born or where we find ourselves living.

Defending the right to emigrate in his 1963 encyclical letter, *Pacem in Terris* ("Peace on Earth"), Blessed John XXIII said:

> That he is a citizen of a particular state does not
> deprive [the human person] of membership to
> the human family, nor of citizenship in that
> universal society, the common, worldwide
> fellowship of men.

The right to emigrate includes obligations. The *Catechism of the Catholic Church* spells these out: "Immigrants are obliged to respect with gratitude the material and spiritual heritage of the country that receives them, to obey its laws and to assist in carrying out civic burdens."

Catholic social doctrine on immigration also recognizes that governments have the duty to control migration into their countries and defend their borders. As guardians of law and order for the common good, governments should consider immigration's impact on their domestic economies and national security. They should set reasonable limits on who they allow to cross their borders, and they can require reasonable documentation and regulate access to public welfare and other services.

But governments must be careful not to use their policies as an excuse to deny decent people the right to seek their livelihood. In this context, Blessed John Paul II cautioned nations never to deny the natural human right to immigration out of exaggerated fears for national security or selfish concerns about threats to domestic jobs or standards of living. The right to emigrate, he said, is part of the "universal common good, which includes the whole family of peoples, beyond every nationalistic egoism."

The Church's *Catechism* states that, as a natural right, immigration imposes obligations upon wealthier nations:

> The more prosperous nations are obliged, to the
> extent they are able, to welcome the *foreigner*
> in search of the security and the means of
> livelihood which he cannot find in his country
> of origin.

Finally, in Catholic teaching, public authorities also have a duty to protect foreign workers from exploitation. The *Compendium of the Social Doctrine of the Church* says that foreign workers must enjoy the "same rights enjoyed by nationals, rights that are to be guaranteed to all without discrimination."

These are the basic principles and concerns that underlie the Church's social doctrine on immigration. Over the centuries, these principles are found consistently in the writings of the Church's saints, popes, and bishops, and also in the authoritative teachings of Church councils, including the Second Vatican Council (1962-1965).

As we notice, these principles don't lead to obvious conclusions on public policy. Immigration is not like the fundamental moral issues of abortion or the defense of the family. In these areas, Catholics' moral obligations are clear and unquestionable. By contrast, there is no single authentic "Catholic position" on immigration.

In our current debates, America's Catholic bishops support a comprehensive reform of our immigration policies that secures our borders and gives undocumented immigrants the chance to earn permanent residency and eventual citizenship. I agree with my brother bishops that this is a sensible and just approach that is in keeping with American principles and values.

I also believe that until we can achieve a comprehensive reform, it makes good sense to impose a moratorium on deportations, except for persons who are guilty of violent or other serious crimes. Because of its grave impact on families, we need to stop deporting people whose only crime is that they are here without the proper papers.

I also think our leaders need to work to encourage economic reforms in Latin America, especially in the region's poorest countries. We need to find ways to target economic development to small business and agriculture so that far fewer Latinos will feel compelled to leave their families to seek jobs and money in other countries. Finally, I think we need to keep pushing for protections of the most vulnerable class of migrants — children and women, who often fall prey to unscrupulous traffickers and others.

This is a time for American Catholic voices and American Catholic witness. Jesus said that to those whom much is given, much will be required. And in this hour of our history, much is required of us as Americans and as Catholics.

If immigrants *are* American history, as historian Oscar Handlin said decades ago, then American Catholics represent a unique subset of the immigrant experience in America. We share the same faith as the missionaries who first charted this land, and we are children of the immigrants who later settled this land. Our Catholic experience in America testifies to the beauty of this nation's founding vision. Our rise from despised immigrants belonging to a suspect religion to positions of leadership in American society should be a sign of hope for today's immigrants.

Our status in American public life gives us a duty. We are called to renew the soul of our nation in the image of her founding beliefs. We have to help our neighbors stay true to America's creed, and to fight for policies that protect the dignity of God's children.

As American Catholics we need to look at this issue in light of our faith in Jesus Christ, and in light of our nation's history, which, we believe, is guided by what America's founders called "divine Providence." In his last book, *Memory and Identity,* finished just before he died in 2005, Blessed John Paul II said: "The history of all nations is called to take its place in the history of salvation."

These words speak to our present moment in America. Our immigration crisis is a crisis of national identity and purpose. Our nation was founded by missionaries to be a "new world" that reflects God's benevolent plan for human history. The national motto chosen by America's founders reflects this same idea — America as a *novus ordo seclorum,* a new order of the ages.

We need to help our neighbors see the immigrants in our midst in light of America's missionary and immigrant heritage. We need to help our neighbors see these new immigrants as part of the story of our nation and part of America's unique place in God's plan for history.

First, we need to be honest with ourselves. We need to remember that despite Catholics' experience as immigrants, some of our ancestors took part in the darker episodes of American history, including slavery, segregation, and, ironically, anti-immigrant bias — especially bias against Mexicans and Latin Americans. Back in the 1860s, Bishop Joseph Machebeuf, the first bishop of

Denver, a courageous French immigrant, had to chastise his flock for their racial attitudes: "You never have a good word for the Mexicans, and you seem to despise them as an inferior race of people."

We need to ask whether these words sometimes can be applied to us today. We need to ask if we have forgotten where we came from, where our parents and grandparents came from. It does seem that some of our hearts have grown cold toward the strangers in our midst. We don't always see them as brothers and sisters, even though most of the undocumented among us share the same baptism as we do. If we knew them, we would know that they are a lot like our ancestors were. They are people with strong traditions of family and faith, community and hard work. I believe the more we get to know them, the more we will want them to be our neighbors, friends, and fellow citizens.

As Catholics, this is an issue that should transcend politics. It's a matter of faith. Since the days of Jesus and the apostles, Catholics have always understood themselves as men and women called to serve God in the poor, in the least of our brothers and sisters. This was the command of Jesus: To love not in words alone, but in deeds. To love in ways that reflect the love that God has for each of his children. To love in truth and self-honesty. To be aware that if we say we love God when we don't love our neighbors we are only lying to ourselves.

In his own ministry, and in his commandments to us, Jesus never distinguished between those who "deserve" our love and those who don't. He told us that God makes his sun to rise on the evil and the good, and sends rain on the just and the unjust. So we can't choose to love some but not to love others. We can't justify showing less compassion for those who don't have the right documents.

Jesus said, "I was a stranger." He did not distinguish between legal and illegal. In fact, he pushed us to find him in those who are the most distressing to us — including strangers and criminals in jail. And we need to remember that he was uncompromising on this point. In the evening of our lives, our love for God will be judged by our love for him in the person of the least among us.

FIVE

THE NEW AMERICA

America is a dream. It always has been. From the beginning.

For the missionaries who migrated here in the sixteenth century, America was a single reality that stretched from the northernmost parts of what is now Canada to the southernmost tip of what is now Argentina. They dreamed that this land was "the end of the earth" and the "new world" that Jesus Christ promised in the Gospels. Their dream was "catholic," or universal. They dreamed of sharing Christ's salvation with the peoples they found here — making them brothers and sisters in the great family of humanity, the divine kingdom that Christ commanded his Church to build on earth.

America's founders dreamed the same dream in a different language. They dreamed of a nation where men and women from every race, creed, and national background could live in equality

— as brothers and sisters, children of the same God. They wrote their dream down in a set of self-evident truth-propositions they called their Declaration of Independence. Like the missionaries before them, they believed their dream was God's dream for the human family.

This is the dream of America. Each of us is a child of the American Dream. We may not know our ancestors' names. Unless we are descended from this land's indigenous peoples, we know that our people did not originate here. For nearly all of us, whoever we are, our ancestors were immigrants. They traveled great distances from some foreign land. Every one of them had a different story. But they all dreamed the same dream. The dream of America.

As children of this dream, this is our inheritance. That inheritance comes to us as a gift. In this hour of American history, this inheritance comes to us also as a duty, because the dream of America is threatened right now — just like so many times before in our history.

The American Dream, as we have seen, has always been a promise not fully delivered, a work in progress. The dream is beautiful and universal. The reality remains painful and partial. We realize that often we haven't lived up to our principles, beginning with America's original sin of slavery and continuing in various forms of nativism and race discrimination.

God has blessed this land and its people with freedom and goodness and generosity. We are a nation of nationalities and many ethnicities, united by a commitment to liberty and equality. The American dream of equality, rooted in the belief in the divine origin of all people, has formed our national conscience and inspired movements for renewal and justice in every generation.

Today the American Dream must inspire a new movement of conscience. This dream must call us to the task of making a new America.

By our political inaction we have allowed a vast underclass to grow at the margins of our society. We have created a situation where millions of men and women are living as perpetual servants — working for low wages in our restaurants and fields; our factories, gardens, homes, and hotels. These men and women have no security against sickness, disability, or old age. In many cases these people can't even open up a checking account or get a driver's license. They serve as our nannies and baby-sitters. But their own children can't get jobs or go to college because they were brought to this country illegally by their parents.

The dream of America was not meant to leave people living in limbo. There are hundreds of thousands being held without charges or representation in "detention centers." Millions more are living with the knowledge that if they make one wrong move they could be arrested, ripped from their families, and locked in those same immigration jails — or deported straight away.

We are the children of immigrants and the children of the American Dream. Is this the best we can do? Can we stand before our ancestors with a clean conscience? Can we stand before God? These are questions each of us must ask. And these are questions for America as a nation.

There are times in the life of a nation that are a trial. We are living in one of those times. Illegal immigration is one of several trials of the next America. How we respond to the challenge of illegal immigration will measure our national character and conscience in this generation. The great debate we are engaged in will tell us if the dream of America still beats in our hearts or whether other dreams have come to take its place.

To be American citizens is a privilege. That privilege demands something of us in this hour. We are being asked to make good on the promise of America. We are being asked to be defenders of this dream that generations have given their lives, fortunes, and sacred honor to defend.

In these pages, I've been trying to reflect on the immigration issue in light of America's history and founding principles, and in light of my own faith tradition as a Catholic.

My point has been that immigration is about more than immigration. I began by suggesting that we need to confront our fears about the "next America." I sketched a spiritual and religious interpretation of American history because I believe we need to know how our history intersects with the Christian mission to Mexico and the other lands of the Americas, the *Nueva España*. I proposed a new appreciation of America's founding creed and its vision of universal brotherhood and sisterhood under the Fatherhood of God. And I have suggested that American Catholics, as heirs to the first missionaries and the first wave of immigrants to this country, have a particular duty in our present debates.

As I said at the start of this little book, I am a pastor of souls, not a politician. I consider politics to be a noble calling that seeks the common good and justice for every individual, especially the poor and most vulnerable. Pastors have a different calling in civic life — to stir hearts and minds, and to form consciences. We want to inspire people to love and serve the poor and to always be close to those in need. We want to motivate people to build a society worthy of the God-given dignity of every person.

In that spirit, in these final pages I want to share some of the conclusions I have come to on this issue, as a Catholic pastor and an American citizen.

I think we need to change the conversation about illegal immigration. We have to stop talking in political categories and using definitions rooted in our own fears. The question of immigration is not about *us* versus *them*. To state the obvious: "illegals" are people just the same as we are.

We all know this in our hearts. But we're not acting like it right now. These days we have our guard up. We seem afraid that we'll go soft on the issue if we remember that these "illegals" are husbands and wives, mothers and fathers, sons and daughters. All with their own stories to tell. All with dreams for their lives and for their children's lives.

This awareness is as fundamental to the Bill of Rights as it is to the Torah and the Sermon on the Mount. In God's eyes we're all his beloved sons and daughters and no one is a stranger to any of us. American democracy is founded on this vision. We know this. Nobody ever forfeits his humanity or his right to be treated with dignity. No matter where he comes from or how he got here. No matter what kind of papers he has or doesn't have. Even if he has broken a law, he is still a person, and he still has rights and dignity.

I realize this sounds naively pious in our agitated political climate. But it's true, and this is no time for polite silence about our values. Too much is at stake to give in to the corrosive cynicism that masks itself as political realism.

Even as I write these words, I can hear the response: "This debate isn't about immigration — it's about *illegal* immigration. It's all well and good for a pastor to speak of illegals being God's children. But they broke our laws. They should've thought about the consequences first. They deserve what they have coming to them. We're only trying to uphold the rule of law."

This is a strong argument, and it's been driving our national conversation and policy for more than a decade. It's hard to argue with the logic. There are millions of immigrants living among us in obvious violation of American law. This makes law-abiding Americans angry, including the many immigrants who played by the rules and entered this country legally. It's also true that letting people get away with breaking our laws brings disorder to society and weakens the social fabric. Our government has not only the right but the responsibility to insist that our laws be respected.

I agree that undocumented immigrants should be held accountable. The question is, How? Right now, we're angry. So almost by default we've made deportation the de facto mandatory sentence for anyone caught without proper documentation. We're not interested in mitigating circumstances or taking into account "hard cases." Illegal immigration may be the only crime for which we don't tolerate plea bargains or lesser sentences. That point alone is worth pondering.

As I listen to our debates, I wonder how much people really know about our immigration laws. How many of us can say we actually know what the laws are and that we understand them? Are we sure that our laws correspond to right reason and the demands of human dignity? Are we sure that our government has been consistent in explaining and enforcing our laws over the years?

I also wonder how much we know about these people we consider so threatening to our security and way of life. Blessed Mother Teresa of Calcutta used to say that everybody likes to *talk about* the poor, but very few people *talk to* the poor. I'm afraid the same is true with undocumented immigrants.

Over the years, in my various ministries as a priest and bishop in Texas, Colorado, and now in Southern California, I've come to know a lot of them. Often, I meet them in church. They are there with their families. They're good people and solid members of their community. They're trying to raise their kids to be good Catholics, and they're trying hard to live their faith themselves.

These men and women have a lot of determination. Most came to this country by traveling hundreds and even thousands of miles on a journey that was hard, dangerous, and demeaning. They left everything they knew behind. Not for a comfortable life, because I meet very few who have achieved that. They came to this country for the same reason our grandparents came — to make a better life for their children. They came for the American Dream.

From my years of ministry and friendship with these newcomers to America, I've concluded that people don't really *choose* to leave their homelands. Emigration is almost always forced upon people by the dire conditions they face in their lives. It may be hunger, violence, or loneliness for a loved one who is on the other side of the border. No one makes this decision lightly. It starts with a desperate feeling that most of us, thank God, will never know — the feeling that any life would be better than the one we're living now.

It can make your heart ache to hear their stories. Women who've given their life savings to "coyotes" who promise to take them across the borders to see their husbands — but instead they take away their money and their dignity, too. It's not easy to get into this country illegally. You have to be willing to walk across deserts that are scorching in the day and freezing at night. You have to be willing to perhaps be stuffed into suffocating train cars and shipping containers. You might be made to crawl through a mile of sewer pipes.

I think we judge these people the wrong way. We don't understand what's driving them. We need to walk a mile in their shoes. Literally. We need to try thinking as they do — as mothers and fathers, as husbands and wives, sons and daughters.

We have to ask ourselves: What wouldn't we do to feed the hungry mouths we are responsible for? What wouldn't we do to be reunited with a loved one? What price wouldn't we pay? And if the law told you that you could never see your children again, would you obey that law?

There is a difficult truth that we have to accept. We

are a nation of laws, as we often say. We are proud of this. And we should be. But for many reasons and for many years, our nation chose not to enforce our immigration laws, or to enforce them only inconsistently. Lax enforcement, of course, doesn't justify people breaking these laws. But it does explain how we reached this crisis where eleven million people are living in our midst without authorization — and most of them have been here for five years or longer.

Our government and law enforcement officials looked the other way because our construction companies, service industries, and farms needed the low-wage labor these immigrants came to offer. That's another difficult truth. Illegal immigration is driven by jobs. When our economy is growing, the "demand" for illegal immigration grows. And the opposite is true. Right now, illegal border crossings are at record lows. In part that's because of better enforcement and border security. It's also because the American economy has been in recession.

Those who come here without authorization come to work, and they form the backbone of key sectors of our economy — agriculture, farming, construction, manufacturing, and leisure and hospitality. Most of them have income taxes withheld from their paychecks — even though they are not eligible for any social benefits.

We need to stop all the false rhetoric about immigrants sneaking into this country to "live off" our welfare system. Everybody who studies these issues knows that's not true. The idea persists because anti-immigrant interests find it to be a useful untruth for stirring up popular resentment. The real truth is that unauthorized immigrants might receive emergency medical treatment, but they have no access to state or federal welfare benefits. It is true, however, that their children, born in this country, are citizens by birth and are entitled to have access to our schools and government programs.

Finally, the evidence strongly suggests that undocumented workers are indeed doing jobs that American workers won't do — either because the pay is too low or the work is too hard, or both. We see this in states that have been cracking down on illegal immigration. Even with unemployment high, businesses can't find enough American citizens willing to fill the jobs being abandoned by undocumented workers who are fleeing the tough new sanctions.

So why don't all these workers just come to America legally?

The first problem is that our national immigration law is actually a complicated web of quotas, queues, caps, and classifications. It's hard to figure out what the law really is. So it takes lawyers, a lot of money, and many years to navigate the legal "alphabet soup" of visa classifications for various kinds of workers.

Then there is our system of "country caps" or national quotas. In an effort to be fair, American immigration law currently limits every country in the world to the same number of visas or "green cards" each year. This rule was put in place in the immigration reform of 1965. The intent was noble — to correct the race-based quota systems that were imposed in the 1920s to bar immigration from Asia and other non-European countries.

The solution was to say that people from every country would have equal access to come to America. But noble intentions have led to sad consequences. Now, every nation in the world — no matter how big or small, no matter how close to America or far away — is allowed the same number of immigrants, about twenty-six thousand each year.

There are many qualifications and technicalities involved, but the basic reality is that the waiting list to get a new visa from Mexico — which shares our border and much of our history — could be ten years or even twenty-five years, depending on what kind of visa you are looking for.

These are the broad outlines of the illegal immigration issue, as I understand it. I am not trying to justify the breaking of our laws. But I think we need to understand these "criminals" and the many circumstances that contributed to their "crime."

If I am right in my understanding of the issues, then we all share a measure of the blame for the problems we face. The result of not enforcing our laws is that millions have been allowed to establish themselves in our communities. They are here working, raising families, paying taxes, doing jobs that need to be done. The rest of us have been benefitting from their work — in the form of lower prices and services that might not otherwise be provided.

It doesn't seem fair for our country not to enforce its laws for many years and then suddenly to start punishing people who broke these laws. It doesn't seem right to break those families up, to start throwing people out of the country — people who came to work and to be with their family; people who have done no harm to anyone.

It also doesn't seem right to make low-wage workers pay huge fines and abandon their families to leave the country to "get back in line" to enter this country legally. Because of the broken logic of our current laws, this process could take more than ten years and thousands of dollars. America can do better than to make people choose between following our law and not seeing their spouses, their children or their relatives for a decade or more.

There are no perfect solutions. Of course, immigration reform depends on continuing to work to secure our borders and finding mechanisms so that we know whom we are letting into our country. In dealing with those who are already here, I think we need a policy that holds them accountable for breaking our laws, but also gives them a chance to normalize their status and invites them to join us as citizens in building the new America. We should consider a kind of statute of limitations — those who have been here for five years or more and have no criminal record should not have to live in fear of deportation.

In terms of penalties, I favor intensive, long-term community service, and civic education and formation. To my mind, this is far more constructive than deportation and fines. This builds families and communities rather than tearing them apart. It teaches respect for our laws at the same time that it helps integrate unauthorized immigrants into America's social fabric.

I have come to the conclusion that immigration reform offers us a special moment as a nation. We have a chance to create a path to welcome millions of new Americans who would share our national ideals, beliefs, and values. They will reinvigorate our economy with a much-needed influx of younger workers committed to hard work, entrepreneurship, and service to our nation.

These are people with energy and aspirations, who are not afraid of making sacrifices. They are people who have courage and the other virtues, and who value God, family, and community.

And already we see that Hispanics are following the pattern of earlier generations of immigrants. They are learning the English language and making sure that their children grow up fluent in English. They are adopting the customs and traditions of the American way of life. They vote. They serve in our military and police forces. They are homeowners and are active in politics.

As immigrants have in every generation, this new generation of immigrants promises to make us a stronger, more virtuous, and prosperous America.

Immigration is about more than immigration. We need to remember this as we try to craft political solutions.

We are finally focused on all the important issues, politically — visa types, country caps, boots on the ground at our borders, new rules and procedures for those who need documentation. But those measures are not enough. As I have tried to argue throughout this book, immigration reform is essentially a religious project, in the original sense of the word — religion as what binds us to ultimate things and connects us to one another.

G. K. Chesterton described America as a "spiritual adventure." What he meant is that America — alone among the nations in history — has been engaged in a historic struggle to build a "cosmic commonwealth" by "molding many peoples into the visible image of the citizen." That is what's at stake in our political discussions about immigration reform.

Right now, we need to rededicate ourselves to this spiritual adventure — to the dream of America's founders and the missionaries who came before them. We need to tell a new American story for a new America. We need to make a new commitment to the American creed. And we need to seek a new "patriotic grace." To carry out this task will take a new unity and sense of solidarity. This unity must be worthy of our missionary and immigrant heritage. It must be based on our founders' dream of America as one nation of freedom and equality under God.

We need to work to make sure that immigration reform is part of an even more comprehensive reform — a project for American renewal aimed at forming a new national identity and civic culture dedicated to the universal values of promoting human dignity, freedom, and a community of the good. We need to take the next steps toward realizing the dream of America.

But in order to achieve this dream, we are going to have to challenge the secularist, multiculturalist, and relativist consensus that in recent decades has taken hold among elite thinkers and opinion-shapers in our universities, cultural centers, and government.

Many of our intellectuals, artists, and political leaders believe strongly that the dream of America was always kind of bogus. According to them, America's founders used their principles and institutions to "mask" their self-interest and protect the privileges of their race, class, and sex. Given their suspicion about America's founding motives, it's not surprising that our elites are skeptical about the ideals of citizenship and integration around a common national identity.

Instead, they envision an America that has no need for any positive definition of citizenship or national identity. They describe a kind of anarchy of diversity; a gathering of peoples from every ethnic background, all freely defining their own self-identities and pursuing their own concepts of the meaning of life, with no obligations to anyone but themselves.

In my opinion, such dreams of America are not capable of nurturing the human ties and sense of duty that we need to make true community possible. Such an America would slide into a general atmosphere of self-indulgence that would only foster new social injustices. This America would be a place where people would pursue their own amusements and selfish interests while care for the poor and concern for the rule of law and the common good would become arbitrary and optional.

If immigration reform is to succeed — if the American dream is to be renewed — we need to reject the mindset of cultural relativism and the careless disregard for American identity. We need to restore the ideal of citizenship based on integration and Americanization. Immigrants should be welcomed within a civic framework built on a common American story and universal values. We should be promoting broad expectations for citizens — including the understanding that individual rights presume common duties; and that freedom doesn't mean doing whatever we want, but instead means doing what is true and beautiful and good.

America's critics are right: Historically, our country has often failed to live up to its principles. But the answer to this is not to shatter the idea of citizenship and national identity into a thousand different opinions and lifestyle enclaves. America is not served by a lazy reflex of anti-Americanism. Neither are the world's poor. A century after Emma Lazarus's poem was fixed to the Statue of Liberty, the world's masses still yearn to breathe free. And they still look to America to lift the torch of freedom.

The answer to America's failures — either in the past or in the future — is to hold up our founding principles and to demand that we live up to them. This has been the attitude of all the true spiritual radicals and reformers in our history, men and women like Orestes Brownson, Dorothy Day, Martin Luther King Jr., César Chávez, and Abraham Joshua Heschel.

Throughout our history, faith in the American Dream has always raised up movements of conscience and renewal, such as the struggle for black civil rights in the 1960s and the farmworkers' movement of the 1970s. We need to renew that faith today.

In his *Letter from Birmingham City Jail* (1963), King wrote:

> One day the South will know that when these
> disinherited children of God sat down at
> lunch counters they were in reality standing
> up for the best in the American dream and
> the most sacred values in our Judeo-Christian
> heritage, and thusly, carrying our whole nation
> back to those great wells of democracy which
> were dug deep by the Founding Fathers in
> the formulation of the Constitution and the
> Declaration of Independence.

King understood what we have been talking about throughout this book — that America was established as a religious project. And as we look toward a new America, we need to return to those sacred values that form the great wells of our democracy.

As we have seen, America's founders based this society on their belief in a Creator who is also the "Supreme Judge of the world." They did not believe democracy could be sustained without shared religious commitments to moral truths — truths about the human person and about society. And they were right.

In recent years, America has departed from its founding beliefs, embarking on an uncharted path — trying to live without reference to God; in fact, excluding all religious considerations from our economic, political, and cultural life.

But we're coming to realize that we can't live without God — not as individuals and not as a society. We're coming to see that when we lose the sense of God, we lose the thread that holds our lives together. We lose the answers to the questions that help us make sense of the world: What kind of person should I be? Why should I be good? What should I believe in? What should I be living for — and why?

Many of our cultural and political leaders today argue that there are no true answers to these questions anyway — just different opinions, beliefs, and preferences. But if they are right, then our future is bleak indeed. Because if they are right, then we truly have no basis for justice and human rights, no foundation for our laws. If our rights don't come from God, then they will depend on whatever the majority decides or on the whims of the government.

This is the greatest danger of the God-free society — that we will lose our reverence for the human person created in God's image. Without God, we have no reason to be our brothers' and sisters' keepers. Without God, we have no reason to fight injustices or to lift up the weak. If God is not there to care, then why should we?

So our work for a new America requires us to challenge the secularization and de-Christianization of our country. We need to have a more mature conversation about what religious freedom means in our democracy. Americans will slways be free not to believe what their neighbors believe. But freedom of religion wasn't meant to keep us free from all possible exposure to our neighbors' beliefs. It wasn't meant to exclude believers or faith-based institutions from participating in our political and public life. America's founders intended religion and government to operate in different spheres, each with their own autonomy and responsibility, and each cooperating for the common good of society. We need to restore religion to its rightful place in American life if we are going to stay true to our founders' dreams of equality and justice for all.

American renewal means building a new America that once more recognizes the sovereignty of God, the sanctity of human life, and the family as the vital cell of society and the first school of virtue. We need to work for an America where life is cherished and welcomed as a gift — from the child in the womb to the elderly and the handicapped, the poor and the prisoner; to the immigrant who comes to our land seeking a new life for his family.

Immigration is about more than immigration. It is about renewing the soul of America. Immigration is about welcoming newcomers into our cultural and political traditions of citizenship. It means teaching them what it means to be an American and what a privilege that is.

We need a new education in civic virtue and citizenship. Our new immigrants need to learn the story of America. Not the story of cynicism and hypocrisy that too often is told in our media and schools, but the true story of America — the story of a people struggling mightily in every generation to live up to the beautiful ideals of the Founding Fathers.

America's story *is* unique and exceptional among the nations of history. We are not a nation that originated in common ties to territory, blood, or kinship. There is no common or preferred race or religion in America. Our identity is spiritual. Americans are not just individuals who occupy the same geographical space. Americans are committed to a dream, to a vision of a world where men and women live in freedom, dignity, and equality. What unites us in all our beautiful diversity of cultures and ways of life is this shared vision of the dignity of the human person created by God.

We need to start teaching that again — first to ourselves, and then to our new immigrants. We need to rediscover and proclaim the noble origins and purposes of America in order to renew the American spirit.

America's history is missionary and immigrant. America was never really a melting pot. America has always been a crossroads and meeting place of cultures — a world city, a cosmopolitan commonwealth. The American creed — with its faith in our common humanity, divine dignity and destiny — is like the frame that holds in place the many pieces of this mosaic of peoples. From the beginning, America has always made room for people from many cultures, speaking different languages, holding different beliefs, customs, and traditions.

Now it is our turn to help make our newest immigrants a part of this great American story. Integration and Americanization mean helping these men and women to join their stories to ours. We need to help them learn our history, our language, and our values. We need to learn from them and inspire them to make their own contributions to the dream of America.

The new America is being determined by the choices we make as believers and as American citizens. By our thoughts and by our words, by what we do and by what we leave undone, we are writing the next chapters of our American story.

FOR FURTHER READING

ONE
THE NEXT AMERICA

Mary Ann Glendon, "Principled Immigration," *First Things* (June/July 2006).

Pew Hispanic Center, *A Nation of Immigrants: A Portrait of the 40 Million, Including 11 Million Unauthorized* (January 29, 2013).

TWO
THE GREATER AMERICA

Carl Anderson and Eduardo Chávez, *Our Lady of Guadalupe: Mother of the Civilization of Love* (Doubleday, 2009).

Ray Allen Billington, *The Protestant Crusade 1800–1860: A Study of the Origins of American Nativism* (Quadrangle, 1964 [1938]).

Herbert Eugene Bolton, *Bolton and the Spanish Borderlands*, ed. J. F. Bannon (University of Oklahoma, 1974).

— "The Epic of Greater America," *American Historical Review*, 38:3 (1933): 448–474.

— *Greater America: Essays in Honor of Herbert Eugene Bolton* (University of California, 1945).

— *Rim of Christendom: A Biography of Eusebio Francisco Kino Pacific Coast Pioneer* (Russell & Russell, 1960).

— *The Spanish Borderlands: A Chronicle of Old Florida and the Southwest* (Yale University, 1921).

Margaret and Stephen Bunson, *Faith in the Wilderness: The Story of the Catholic Indian Missions* (Our Sunday Visitor, 2000).

Eduardo Chávez, *Our Lady of Guadalupe and Saint Juan Diego: The Historical Evidence* (Rowman & Littlefield, 2006).

Fredi Chiappelli, Michael J. B Allen, and Robert L. Benson, eds. *First Images of America: The Impact of the New World on the Old*, 2 vols. (University of California, 1976).

Donald E. Chipman, *Spanish Texas, 1519–1821* (University of Texas, 1992).

Joseph F. Chorpenning, ed., *Joseph of Nazareth through the Centuries* (Saint Joseph's University, 2011).

— *Patron Saint of the New World: Spanish American Colonial Images of Saint Joseph* (Saint Joseph's University, 1992).

Joseph F. Chorpenning and Barbara Von Barghahn, *The Holy Family as Prototype of the Civilization of Love: Images from the Viceregal Americas* (Saint Joseph's University, 1996).

Christopher Columbus, *The Four Voyages of Christopher Columbus* (Penguin, 1969).

— *The Log of Christopher Columbus* (International Marine, 1992).

Virgil Elizondo, ed., *Way of the Cross: The Passion of Christ in the Americas* (Rowman & Littlefield, 2002).

John Tracy Ellis, *Catholics in Colonial America* (Helicon, 1965).

Marilyn H. Fedewa, *María of Ágreda: Mystical Lady in Blue* (University of New Mexico, 2010).

Carlos Fernández-Shaw, *The Hispanic Presence in North America: From 1492 to Today* (Facts on File, 1991).

Carlos Fuentes, *The Buried Mirror: Reflections on Spain and the New World* (Houghton Mifflin, 1992).

Margaret C. Galitzin, *Ven. Mary of Agreda in America* (Tradition in Action, 2011).

Michael V. Gannon, *The Cross in the Sand: The Early Catholic Church in Florida, 1513–1870* (University Press of Florida, 1983 [1965]).

Maynard J. Geiger, O. F. M., *The Life and Times of Fray Junípero Serra, O. F. M., or the Man Who Never Turned Back* (Academy of American Franciscan History, 1959).

John Gilmary Shea, *The Catholic Church in Colonial Days* (Edward O. Jenkins' Sons, 1886).

Frederick W. Hodge and Theodore H. Lewis, eds., *Spanish Explorers in the Southern United States, 1528–1543* (Texas State Historical Association, 1985).

R. Po-Chia Hsia, *The World of Catholic Renewal, 1540–1770* (Cambridge, 1998).

Pierre Janelle, *The Catholic Reformation* (Bruce, 1949).

John F. Kennedy, *A Nation of Immigrants* (Harper Perennial, 2008 [1964]).

Jacques Lafaye, *Quetzalcóatl and Guadalupe: The Formation of Mexican National Consciousness, 1531–1813* (University of Chicago, 1976).

Jaime Lara, "The First Church Dedicated to St. Joseph in the New World: An Aztec-Christian Chapel in Mexico City," in *Joseph of Nazareth through the Centuries,* ed. F. Chorpenning (Saint Joseph's University, 2011), 241–262.

Timothy Matovina, *Guadalupe and Her Faithful: Latino Catholics in San Antonio, from Colonial Origins to the Present* (Johns Hopkins, 2005).

Samuel Eliot Morison, *Admiral of the Ocean Sea: A Life of Christopher Columbus* (Little, Brown, 1942).

M. N. L. Couve de Murville, *The Man Who Founded California: The Life of Blessed Junípero Serra* (Ignatius, 2000).

Albert J. Nevins, M.M., *Our American Catholic Heritage* (Our Sunday Visitor, 1972).

Nothingness Itself: Selected Writings of Ven. Fr. Antonio Margil, 1690–1724 (Franciscan Herald, 1976).

Marvin R. O'Connell, *The Counter Reformation, 1560–1610* (Harper, 1974).

Edmundo O'Gorman, *The Invention of America: An Inquiry into the Historical Nature of the New World and the Meaning of Its History* (Greenwood, 1972 [1948]).

Francisco Palou, *Francisco Palou's Life and Apostolic Labors of the Venerable Junípero Serra* (Applewood, n.d. [1913]).

Octavio Paz, *The Labyrinth of Solitude and Other Writings* (Grove, 1985).

Robert Ricard, *The Spiritual Conquest of Mexico: An Essay on the Apostolate and the Evangelizing Methods of the Mendicant Order in New Spain, 1523-1572* (University of California, 1966).

Francis J. Weber, *A Bibliographical Gathering: The Writings of Msgr. Francis J. Weber, 1953-1993* (McNally and Loftin, 1995).

— *California's Catholic Heritage* (Dawson's, 1974).

— *Catholic Church in California* (Saint Francis Historical Society, 1997).

— *A History of the Archdiocese of Los Angeles and its Precursor Jurisdictions in Southern California, 1840-2007* (Archdiocese of Los Angeles, 2007).

— *Vignettes of California Catholicism* (Mission Hills, 1988).

THREE

AMERICAN CREED

Tyler Anbinder, *Nativism and Slavery: The Northern Know Nothings and the Politics of the 1850s* (Oxford University, 1992).

Carl Becker, *The Declaration of Independence: A Study in the History of Political Ideas* (Vintage, 1958).

Lynn Bridgers, *Death's Deceiver: The Life of Joseph P. Machebeuf* (University of New Mexico, 1997).

Dietrich Bonhoeffer, *Ethics* (Touchstone, 1995 [1949]).

G. K. Chesterton, *What I Saw in America* (Hodder & Stoughton, 1922).

J. Hector St. John de Crèvecoeur, *Letters from an American Farmer and Sketches of Eighteenth-Century America* (Penguin, 1981).

Oscar Handlin, *The Uprooted: The Epic Story of the Great Migrations that Made the American People* (Little, Brown, 1973 [1951]).

Samuel P. Huntington, *Who Are We? The Challenges to America's National Identity* (Simon & Schuster, 2004).

Martin Luther King, Jr., *Where Do We Go from Here: Chaos or Community* (Beacon, 2010 [1967]).

Jacques Maritain, *Reflections on America* (Scribner's, 1958).

Vincent Phillip Muñoz, *God and the Founders: Madison, Washington and Jefferson* (Cambridge, 2009).

John Courtney Murray, S. J., *We Hold These Truths: Catholic Reflections on the American Proposition* (Image, 1964 [1960]).

Philip Wayne Powell, *Tree of Hate: Propaganda and Prejudices Affecting United States Relations with the Hispanic World* (Basic, 1971).

Clinton Rossiter, *Seedtime of the Republic: The Origin of the*

American Tradition of Political Liberty (Harcourt, Brace, 1953).

Shelby Steele, *The Content of Our Character: A New Vision of Race in America* (Harper Perennial, 1998 [1991]).

Alexis de Tocqueville, *Democracy in America*, 2 vols. (The Library of America, 2004).

Ernest Lett Tuveson, *Redeemer Nation: The Idea of America's Millennial Role* (University of Chicago, 1968).

--------- ⭐ ---------

FOUR

CATHOLICS IN AMERICA

David Batson, *The Treasure Chest of the Early Christians: Faith, Care and Community from the Apostolic Age to Constantine the Great* (Eerdmans, 2001).

J. Brian Benestad, *Church, State, and Society: An Introduction to Catholic Social Doctrine* (Catholic University of America, 2010).

The Catechism of the Catholic Church, 2nd. ed. (Liberia Editrice Vatican, 1997), no. 2241 (on immigration).

James Hennesy, S. J., *American Catholics: A History of the Roman Catholic Community in the United States* (Oxford, 1981).

Charles R. Morris, *American Catholic: The Saints and Sinners Who Built America's Most Powerful Church* (Vintage, 1997).

Pontifical Council for Justice and Peace, *Compendium of the*

Social Doctrine of the Church (Washington, DC: USCCB Publishing, 2005), nos. 297–298 (on immigration).

Pope Pius XII, *Exsul Familia Nazarethana,* apostolic constitution on the spiritual care of migrants (August 1, 1952).

Christine D. Pohl, *Making Room: Recovering Hospitality as a Christian Tradition* (Eerdmans, 1999).

Michael Schwartz, *The Persistent Prejudice: Anti-Catholicism in America* (Our Sunday Visitor, 1984).

Rodney Stark, *The Rise of Christianity* (HarperCollins, 1997).

Giulivo Tessarolo, P. S. S. C., *Exsul Familia: The Church's Magna Charta for Migrants* (Saint Charles Seminary, 1962).

United States Conference of Catholic Bishops, *Welcoming The Stranger Among Us: Unity In Diversity* (November 15, 2000)

United States Conference of Catholic Bishops and Bishops Conference of Mexico, *Strangers No Longer: Together on the Journey of Hope* (January 22, 2003)

---- ★ ----

FIVE

THE NEW AMERICA

Bishops of Latin America and the Caribbean, Fifth General Conference Concluding Document (Aparecida, Brazil, May 13–31, 2007).

Gregory S. Butler, *In Search of the American Spirit: The Political*

Thought of Orestes Brownson (Southern Illinois University, 1992).

M. Daniel Carroll R., *Christians at the Border: Immigration, the Church and the Bible* (Baker, 2008).

Jeff Chenoweth and Laura Burdick, *A More Perfect Union: A National Citizenship Plan* (Catholic Legal Immigration Network, 2007)

Frederick John Dalton, *The Moral Vision of César Chávez* (Orbis, 2003).

Andrew Delbanco, *The Real American Dream: A Meditation on Hope* (Harvard, 1999).

Ross Douthat, *Bad Religion: How We Became a Nation of Heretics* (Free Press, 2012).

Brad S. Gregory, *The Unintended Reformation: How a Religious Revolution Secularized Society* (Harvard Belknap, 2012).

Jane Guskin and David L. Wilson, *The Politics of Immigration: Questions and Answers* (Monthly Review, 2007).

Alfred T. Hennelly, S. J., *Santo Domingo and Beyond: Documents and Commentaries from the Historic Meeting of the Latin American Bishops' Conference* (Orbis, 1993).

James K. Hoffmeier, *The Immigration Crisis: Immigrants, Aliens, and the Bible* (Crossway, 2009).

Paul Hollander, *Anti-Americanism: Critiques at Home and Abroad, 1965–1990* (Oxford, 1992).

Blessed John Paul II, *Ecclesia in America*, post-synodal apostolic exhortation on the Encounter with the Living Jesus Christ, the Way to Conversion, Communion and Solidarity in America (January 22, 1999).

— *Memory and Identity: Conversations at the Dawn of the Millennium* (Rizzoli, 2005).

— *Make Room for the Mystery of God: Visit of John Paul II to the USA 1995* (Pauline, 1995).

— *The Pope Speaks to the American Church* (HarperCollins, 1992).

Donald Kerwin and Jill Marie Gerschutz, eds., *And You Welcomed Me: Migration and Catholic Social Teaching* (Lexington, 2009).

Martin Luther King Jr., *A Testament of Hope: The Essential Writings and Speeches of Martin Luther King Jr.* (HarperCollins, 1991).

Peggy Noonan, *Patriotic Grace: What It Is and Why We Need It Now* (HarperCollins, 2008).

Richard John Neuhaus, *American Babylon: Notes of a Christian Exile* (Basic, 2009).

Pia M. Orrenius and Madeline Zavodny, *Beside the Golden Door: U.S. Immigration Reform in a New Era of Globalization* (American Enterprise Institute, 2010).

United States Department of State, Bureau of Consular Affairs, *Visa Bulletin*, 9:58 (July 2013). http//:travel.state.gov/visa/bulletin/bulletin_5993.html

About the Author

──────────── ✭ ────────────

Most Reverend José H. Gomez is Archbishop of Los Angeles, the nation's largest Catholic community. He is the Chairman of the United States Conference of Catholic Bishops' Committee on Migration and a consultant to the Pontifical Commission for Latin America. Archbishop Gomez has written two books: *Men of Brave Heart: The Virtue of Courage in the Priestly Life* (Our Sunday Visitor, 2009) and *A Will to Live: Clear Answers on End of Life Issues* (Basilica, 2006). His writings have been published in *L'Osservatore Romano, First Things*, and elsewhere. Archbishop Gomez is a native of Monterrey, Mexico, and a naturalized American citizen. His writings, speeches, and homilies are available at www.archbishopgomez.com.